Dr. David Winter's medical practice is one of the most prestigious, successful concierge practices in the country. As a founder and leader of HealthTexas Provider Network, Baylor Scott & White Health's affiliated medical group, Dr. Winter has demonstrated time and time again that he is a visionary and innovator with respect to the practice of medicine. When Dr. Winter talks, doctors should listen.

Nathan S. Kaufman
Managing Director
Kaufman Strategic Advisors, LLC

In a time of constant change, the health care industry needs more leaders like Dr. Winter. Service Extraordinaire *provides a real-life case study of a creative—and effective—care model, concierge medicine, and how it can positively impact physicians and patients alike. As a longtime colleague and patient of Dr. Winter, I have experienced firsthand the passion and dedication he has for medicine and his patients. His successful commitment to innovating patient care is a role model example of what's working well in health care.*

B. G. Porter
CEO
Studer Group, a Huron Solution

Service Extraordinaire *will be of great interest to patients and physicians who are dissatisfied with the way they are currently receiving or providing medical care. Dr. David Winter is well qualified to explain how concierge medicine might, or might not, meet the needs of such patients or physicians. His insight is based on being the medical director of 1,300 medical providers, and by his experience as a practicing concierge physician for many years. As defined by Dr. Winter, the main attraction of concierge medicine to both patient and physician is based on a retainer fee that allows immediate physician access to patients in an unrushed manner. There is a strong emphasis on maintenance of good health through proper lifestyle. However, this book also makes it clear that another important factor in concierge medicine is that the doctor has sound medical judgment and deep and sustained knowledge of all aspects of internal medicine, so that medical illnesses are promptly diagnosed and appropriately treated, both in an office setting and in high-intensity hospital settings. Unfortunately, it is difficult for patients to obtain an accurate measure of a doctor's sustained clinical knowledge and medical judgment.*

John S. Fordtran, MD
Director of Gastrointestinal Physiology
Baylor University Medical Center

In today's consumer-oriented health care system, there is no more "one size fits all." In fact, the pressures to customize around the needs and desires of our patients have never been greater. Concierge medicine is the ultimate expression of segmentation and focus. In a world where we must think of an "N of one" versus an "N of many," and must find ways to capitalize on the opportunities afforded by our uniqueness, this model is critical to our success.

Jim Hinton
CEO
Baylor Scott & White Health

Service Extraordinaire
Unlocking the Value of
Concierge Medicine

Service Extraordinaire
Unlocking the Value of
Concierge Medicine

One Physician's Journey into a New
Model of Care
By
F. David Winter Jr., MD, MSc, MACP

CRC Press
Taylor & Francis Group
Boca Raton London New York

CRC Press is an imprint of the
Taylor & Francis Group, an **informa** business

A PRODUCTIVITY PRESS BOOK

CRC Press
Taylor & Francis Group
6000 Broken Sound Parkway NW, Suite 300
Boca Raton, FL 33487-2742

International Standard Book Number-13: 978-1-138-03558-4 (Hardback)
International Standard Book Number-13: 978-1-315-26692-3 (eBook)

Library of Congress Cataloging-in-Publication Data

Names: Winter, F. David, author.
Title: Service extraordinaire : unlocking the value of concierge medicine / F. David Winter.
Description: Boca Raton : Taylor & Francis, 2018. | Includes bibliographical references and index.
Identifiers: LCCN 2017035959| ISBN 9781138035584 (hardback : alk. paper) | ISBN 9781315266923 (ebook)
Subjects: LCSH: Medicine--Practice. | Medical care--Finance.
Classification: LCC R728 .W615 2018 | DDC 610.68/1--dc23
LC record available at https://lccn.loc.gov/2017035959

Visit the Taylor & Francis Web site at
http://www.taylorandfrancis.com

and the CRC Press Web site at
http://www.crcpress.com

I dedicate this book to my loving wife and lifelong companion, Reneé, and to our children, Dave and Brittany, who continue to bring joy and happiness to us both.

The landscape of concierge medicine is growing and changing rapidly. Historically, concierge medicine catered to a small, generally affluent, segment of patients who wanted, and were willing to pay for, more personalized attention. Today, however, both patients and providers are actively seeking new care models that meet their changing needs: patients are spending more of their own money on care, and thus are more attentive to their care experience; providers, burned out by ever-increasing demands on their schedule, are seeking opportunities to reset the pace and focus of their work.

The Advisory Board Company
(Advisory Board)

Contents

Preface

In the Beginning: A Journey into Concierge Medicine

I began the private practice of internal medicine a little over 30 years ago. While I started medical school with an interest in the surgical field, the mystery-solving aspect of internal medicine emphasized by Dr. William Dietz, the chief of Internal Medicine at the University of Texas Medical Branch at Galveston during my student years, drew me into a field that I continue to find stimulating and fascinating.

I, likewise, didn't start my career in internal medicine with the intention of running a concierge medicine practice. On completing my internal medicine internship and residency training at Baylor University Medical Center in Dallas, Texas, I first considered joining the staff of one of the four dominant internal medicine groups at the time, but ultimately decided to start my own practice. I did this in the time-honored tradition of having my dad come to town to help me set up. I had reserved two weeks to prepare my office, arranging furniture and setting up filing cabinets, and had anticipated a slow start. We were both surprised when the phone began ringing repeatedly for appointments almost as soon as the announcements of the practice opening went out. By the end of the fourth day, my first two weeks were booked, and my father left, saying, "You won't have time for me, so I will get out of your hair."

My practice grew quickly, and the next year I brought in a partner, Dr. Paul Muncy. Our two-physician practice continued to grow into the early 1990s, when new challenges began to arise. Insurance companies, upon which private practitioners depend for payments, started consolidating. This gave them more leverage, which they began to assert. When insurers began telling us how many blood tests, x-rays, and electrocardiograms we could order, many of us became concerned about interference with our ability to care for patients. Together with 20 like-minded internal medicine physicians, Dr. Muncy and I started to explore alternatives. Enthusiasm and ideas seemed strong at first, but waned after nine months. Concerned over the lack of progress, I engaged the services of a lawyer and an accountant, and, together with Dr. Muncy, put together a set of bylaws for a new physician organization. I named the group MedProvider, influenced by a popular song at the time, Soul Provider. Initially 17 physicians signed on, and, from there, the practice grew. By 1993, we were discussing affiliation with two other physician groups in the Dallas area—discussions which Boone Powell Jr., then-chief executive officer of Baylor Health Care System, asked to join.

Physician employment by hospitals was not popular at the time, and negotiations went back and forth over many months. Ultimately, however, we agreed that the complementary nature of hospitals and physicians meant that alignment with a hospital system whose leaders and representatives we trusted was in the best interests for everyone—physicians, hospitals, and, of course, our patients. The result was the formation of HealthTexas Provider Network (HTPN)—a single-member 501(a) physician organization (with Baylor Health Care System as the single member) formed under the Texas Medical Practice Act. This law prohibits corporate medical groups in the state unless the group's board consists of physicians in the "full time practice of medicine" (Advisory Board Company, 2016).

The success of this venture can be seen in HTPN as it exists in 2017: a multispecialty, fee-for-service medical group, headquartered in Dallas that employs more than 1,300 providers practicing in more than 350 care delivery sites across North Texas, including 121 primary care centers, and reporting more than three million patient visits in the past fiscal year (HealthTexas Provider Network). I currently serve as the president and chairman of the board of HTPN and am very proud to say that it has been a leader in health care quality improvement and patient-centered care since its founding in 1994—including winning the American Medical Group Association (AMGA) Medical Group Preeminence Award in 2010, as well as being an AMGA Acclaim Award Honoree in 2011, 2012, and 2014 (HealthTexas Provider Network). Much of HTPN's success is attributable to the collaborative relationship established and fostered between the physicians and Baylor Health Care System administrators—in particular, Boone Powell Jr., his successor Joel Allison, and Gary Brock, the current chief integrated delivery network officer for Baylor Scott & White Health (formed through the 2013 merger between Baylor Health Care System and Scott & White Healthcare).

My experience with HTPN—particularly with respect to the high quality of care achieved through the collaborative work of the physicians organized within this group—stimulated my interest in other models of care that offered similar opportunities to improve the patient experience. One of these models, which two of my partners and I traveled to Seattle, Washington, to explore in 2000, was concierge medicine. At the time, concierge practices appeared to be flourishing in Seattle, with both patients and physicians embracing the model as a solution to the problems surrounding access to care with traditional medicine practices in that part of the country. Patients were having difficulty obtaining appointments, while the physicians were overworked and frustrated.

Dallas was not, at the time, in the same predicament so, while we observed the concierge model with interest, we saw no immediate demand for it within HTPN.

Fast-forwarding to 2010, however, the situation had changed. In my own practice, overwork had become a reality as I devoted long hours to my dual roles as a full-time physician with the large panel of patients typical of a fee-for-service medical practice, and as chairman and president of HTPN. I remember working long hours as I juggled my large panel of patients with my administrative duties. The work was fulfilling, but my wife made the point that we were not spending much time together. In looking for a solution, I was confronted with a dilemma: either give up my private practice or step down from my administrative roles.

Non-physicians may not appreciate the joys and rewards of solving an obscure diagnosis, helping a patient through a significant illness, or comforting those at the end of their lives. I was not ready to forego those experiences. I was also quite proud of the physician organization that I had helped build and did not want to leave it. Recalling my visit to Seattle, the solution to my dilemma became apparent. Instead of choosing between administration and a private practice, there was a third option. I could reduce my clinical practice by pioneering the first concierge practice within Baylor Health Care System. By doing so, I figured that I could cut back to a smaller panel of patients, thus leaving time both for my administrative responsibilities and my family.

When I first approached Baylor Health Care System senior executives with the idea, it was met with consternation. There were other existing concierge practices in North Texas, though none were affiliated with a health care system, leaving the question of how a concierge practice would fit into a not-for-profit, mission-driven health care organization. Additionally, with an existing shortage of primary care physicians, would establishing a practice premised on smaller panel sizes further strain access for the community we served? And how would other physicians feel about a concierge practice, with the model's implications of exclusivity and a tiered medical system?

To answer these questions, Baylor Health Care System appointed a committee of respected senior executives, comprising the chief executive officer, chief operating officer, chief strategy officer, chief legal officer, and president of the foundation. Issues considered included:

- Panel sizes of primary care physicians were growing, displeasing both patients and physicians.
- Primary care physicians were under pressure to see more patients.
- An important constituency of clients wanted extra attention and was willing to pay for it.
- Physicians wanted to spend more time with their patients.
- Demand for concierge practices was being met elsewhere in the marketplace.
- There was a correlation of concierge patients with philanthropic grants.

> Personal communication with Rowland K. Robinson, President, Baylor Health Care System Foundation, 7 June 2017 (Robinson, 2017)

After careful and diligent consideration, the committee concluded that concierge medicine could indeed play a role in our system. With this blessing, I began the transition from my traditional fee-for-service practice within MedProvider to a newly established concierge practice—named "Signature Medicine." Leaving my patients of many years was not something that I relished. Letters were sent to my approximately 3,000 private practice patients, all mailed on the same day, offering them the opportunity to join a limited panel of 300 patients in a concierge model. It did not take long to fill all 300 slots, but this still meant ending my relationship with more than 2,500 of my patients. Many were reluctant to see me go, and the partings were often emotional on both sides. Most expressed understanding of my need to cut back on my clinical hours, and the weeks prior to my new practice's start date brought a stream of grateful patients bearing gifts and congratulations. Those who joined my new concierge practice were excited about the new idea. Those who did not join expressed support for my decision but were often tearful as they talked about the good times that we had experienced together. There were, of course, some who expressed frustration with my decision, including those who explicitly did not want to pay extra for services that they were accustomed to receiving.

My physician partners also had mixed feelings. Many applauded what they considered a formidable proposition to balance the work between patient care and physician leadership. Several liked the idea and saw advantages in continuing to experience the intricacies of clinical work, which would give insight to my administrative role. While no one explicitly criticized my move to concierge medicine, I am sure there were colleagues who harbored these concerns.

For me, the balance between a concierge medical practice and my administrative duties works well. Currently, I reserve mornings for patient appointments and perform administrative duties in the afternoons. There is crossover, and I have been known to respond to administrative issues in between patients in the mornings. I have also seen patients in my separate administrative office in the afternoons.

Primary care physicians who are challenged with multiple leadership roles yet still enjoy direct interactions with patients may find the concierge model appealing. Physicians who feel like they are on a treadmill and cannot control the demand for their services, and those who are exhausted and not enjoying their work anymore may all find relief in this alternative practice model. This practice style may not be suited to everyone, but it has brought back the joy of medicine to those who have made this work for them and their patients.

Patients who are less than satisfied with their current doctor–physician relationship may be attracted to the concierge model. The chapters here can demonstrate some of the advantages and attributes. Savvy observers of our health care system will recognize many of the lessons here are applicable to non-concierge practices.

Leaders of hospital systems can learn what concierge models bring to their enterprise. This includes the capture and retention of patients when hospitals support these new models.

Foreword

Health care is on everybody's minds today for a variety of reasons, including questions such as, "How can I be sure I will have access to quality care that is affordable, and will I be able to get and keep a physician?"

There is no question that we are in the midst of a very rapidly changing health care environment, including the national discussion and debate on how health care will be delivered, how it will be paid for, and who will pay for it.

While it is true that there is a great deal of uncertainty in the health care environment today, this has allowed for significant innovation and disruption. Providers are continually exploring the most efficient and effective ways to deliver high-quality, affordable care to patients. Physicians are especially involved in this space.

It has been a long-held belief by many that the patient–physician relationship is one of the most sacred. However, health care consumers and physicians have become very frustrated because they see this relationship becoming increasingly disrupted by insurance companies, governmental payers, and an abundance of (perhaps outdated) rules and regulations.

Dr. David Winter provides the reader of this book a very detailed overview and background about one model of patient care that attempts to preserve the patient–physician relationship. The model he describes is known as concierge medicine.

Concierge medicine is a relatively new concept that first emerged in Seattle in 1996, but has continued to grow and expand as a new model of care over the past 20 years.

With the changes and disruption in health care today being driven by forces like regulations, economics, technology, and consumerism, Dr. Winter does a masterful job of explaining how concierge medicine has emerged as one response to these forces.

Many of today's health care consumers want their care delivered when they want it, how they want it, and where they want it. At the same time, the technological changes and disruptions that are occurring allow patients to take more control of their care and choose models of care such as concierge medicine.

Dr. Winter candidly chronicles his own personal journey to concierge medicine, beginning with his opening a private practice following his residency. The next step was adding a partner, then forming a large medical group, and eventually becoming a part of a large health care system.

But as he experienced the added burden of regulations and paperwork, decreased time with his patients, and additional administrative duties as chairman of HealthTexas Provider Network, an employed physician division of Baylor Scott & White Health, he began considering concierge medicine.

Dr. Winter frankly discusses the pros and cons of concierge medicine, including his own personal struggle, knowing he would be reducing his patient panel significantly and that many would not choose to follow him into his concierge medicine practice because of financial concerns. He also points out the considerable concern and debate as to how this type of model would function within a faith-based, mission-driven organization. Dr. Winter explains the process as to how the decision was ultimately made in a manner designed to help maintain the mission of the system.

As long as there are patients who desire this type of model and the increasing concern of being able to get and keep a primary care physician, concierge medicine will continue to be one of the options offered. But again, as stated in this book, it is just one option among others, as obviously concierge medicine is not for everyone. However, the challenge will be the type of options offered, as consumers want choice.

The book is instructive to physicians considering a concierge medicine practice, as well as to chief executive officers and other top leaders of non-profit health care systems, as it demonstrates an additional option for the patients that they serve.

The concern around and fear of creating a two-tiered system of health care is understandable, and unless there is an intelligent and workable solution coming from our elected officials that allows all patients to have access to safe, quality, affordable health care, that concern will continue, and there will be those who want the choice of concierge medicine.

One reason: it is one emerging model that seeks to maintain the sacred patient–physician relationship. Dr. Winter's very candid and thought-provoking book is definitely worth reading.

Joel Allison, MS
Former CEO of Baylor Scott & White Health

Prologue

Health care in America is changing. Like it or not, health care in this country in the future is going to be different. It may be better in some ways and worse in others, but it will definitely be different.

The reasons for change are multiple. Chief among them is the increasing complexity of modern medicine. Problems that years ago were handled by a solo practitioner now commonly require a team of providers. The outcomes can be quite a bit better but increased efforts, specialization, and collaboration are required.

Clayton M. Christensen and his colleagues in *The Innovator's Prescription* pronounced our health care system as having "unfathomable, interdependent technological and economic complexity" and stated that "health care is a terminal illness for America's governments and business." Christensen's proposition was that our health care industry is ripe for disruption, and will either change itself, or sit back and let someone else lead the change (Christensen et al., 2009).

Concierge medicine is a disruptor to our traditional health care model. It is also well suited to mitigate many of the challenges related to the complexity of modern medicine, and address the chronic nature of many of the diseases that represent the greatest health care burdens for the U.S. population in the 21st century.

Take, for example, congestive heart failure. In the not-too-distant past, the five-year mortality from heart failure was more than 50%, but today, people with this condition can live for decades, though focused attention from a multidisciplinary team involving dietitians, pharmacists, nurses, care coordinators, and both primary care and specialty physicians is required (Braunwald, 2013). Treatment options and strategies include medications, dietary restrictions, surgery, heart muscle assist devices, pacemakers, and stem cell injections. Guiding an individual patient through this maze of options and associated providers to develop and coordinate an individualized treatment strategy requires a knowledgeable navigator—especially as several of the treatment options require close monitoring and frequent adjustments. This navigation role is commonly assigned to the primary care physician, but it is challenging in the context of a typical, busy, fee-for-service practice that allows only 15 minutes for an office visit. Concierge medicine—with its smaller patient panel sizes and emphasis on access and focused, unrushed appointment—allows physicians both the time and attention needed for effective coordination and oversight of such complex care (Gunderman, 2016).

Concierge medicine, like many types of medical practices, comes in many different flavors, offering different styles and emphases. It also does not operate in isolation, and lessons learned in the concierge setting can be applied to improve other aspects of health care delivery. This book is intended to address the many facets of concierge medicine, including why this form of medicine developed in the first place, what types of patients and physicians are attracted to it, how to optimize the discipline, and advantages it can offer for health care systems, physicians, and patients.

Acknowledgments

Each day, I have the privilege of working with my colleagues in Signature Medicine, who embrace our innovative approach to practicing medicine designed around patients and focused on personalized service and individualized attention. Crystal Abbott, Gwen Denbow, Carolyn House, and Reneé Winter (my number 1 wife and number 2 nurse) make it their daily goal to deliver the very best care to everyone that we serve. I am honored to work with them.

I am also grateful to my patients, who have been teaching me about the importance of delivering high-quality, patient-centered care since I began practicing medicine over 30 years ago.

The idea for this book came from my dyadic partner, Sarah Gahm, who observed our receipt of numerous national, top service excellence awards, and posed the innocent question, "What are you doing different in your clinic?" Her observation was that there must be "teachable moments" and her directive was "you should write a book."

Role models and mentors have shaped my thoughts and career, and I am privileged to have learned from John Fordtran, Ralph Tompsett, Michael Emmett, Boone Powell Jr., and Bill Aston.

The following have also been instructive and have contributed to the success of our institution: Gary Brock, John McWhorter, Doug Lawson, Jim Hinton, David Ballard, Cliff

Fullerton, Carl Couch, Paul Muncy, Paul Madeley, Michael Massey, Brent Walker, Glenn Ledbetter, Goran Klintmalm, Jim Fleshman, Richard Naftalis, Butch Derrick, John Bousquet, Jennifer Zimmer, Jane Ensey, Amy Wilson, Sharon Tucker, Craig Kneten, Michael Sills, Gary Hoss, John Mercer, Alan Jones, Loree Lieving, Kevin Liu, Cathy Raver, Michael Rothkopf, Michael Valachovic, Eric Beshires, Ken Katzen, Alyssa Endres, and Cindy DeCoursin. Joel Allison, Steve Boyd, Robin Robinson, and Bill Roberts have done likewise and also served as the advisory board to the formation of Signature Medicine.

In addition, I am appreciative of the efforts of Briget da Graca, Nanette Myers, Kathleen Richter, and Alyssa Turner, who provided expert editorial support for the production of this book.

About the Author

F. David Winter, Jr, MD, MSc, MACP is the president and chairman of the Board of HealthTexas Provider Network (HTPN), a 1,300+ physician organization in partnership with Baylor Scott & White Health, the largest not-for-profit health care system in Texas. Dr. Winter provides oversight to all HTPN clinical operations and ensures the continued development of disease management protocols and quality initiatives. Dr. Winter also provides direction and support to HTPN senior leadership and the HTPN medical directors, collaborating with medical and clinical leadership for prioritization of clinical care redesign, clinical integration, and physician integration strategies. In addition, Dr. Winter serves as a champion for managing illness, coordinating care, and optimizing the health and wellness of the patient population.

Dr. Winter also leads Signature Medicine, an innovative approach to practicing medicine designed around patients subscribing to enhanced health care services, focused on personalized service and individualized attention. As a physician practicing concierge medicine, Dr. Winter is able to offer his patients enhanced one-on-one communication, total access, and a commitment to providing safe, quality, and compassionate health care.

Dr. Winter graduated from the University of Texas Medical Branch in Galveston and is board certified in internal medicine. He has been affiliated with Baylor Healthcare

System, now part of Baylor Scott & White Health, since the late 1970s, when he completed his internship and residency at Baylor University Medical Center at Dallas. He has also been elected to Mastership in the American College of Physicians. Dr. Winter was an original founder and president of MedProvider, a premier group of internal medicine specialists, and in 1994, he led the group into its merger with other physician groups, including the system that formed HTPN. Thereafter, he co-founded the Quality Improvement Committee and served as its chairman for the first eight years.

Dr. Winter earned a master of science in medical management from the University of Texas at Dallas in 2000. As Chairman of the Board of HTPN, he was honored, along with the organization, as a recipient of the 2008 Top Leadership Team in Healthcare Award for medical group practices, the 2016 Health Ethics Trust award, and numerous awards from the American Medical Group Association.

Chapter 1

The Concierge Model

What Is Concierge Medicine?

Concierge medicine, boutique medicine, membership medicine, retainer fee medicine ... all refer to a novel way to deliver health care. Extra fees, extra attention, and extraordinary service are a part of this new field of medicine. Upfront payments, called retainer fees, change the business model of physician practices. No longer is there a need to be concerned about a daily quota of patients or procedures, as in a fee-for-service model. In fact, the total number of patients in the panel is typically capped so that a physician is prevented from the rushed, never-enough-time style of practice that many of today's physicians experience.

The economics of the concierge model are built around the retainer fee, an additional charge that supports the practice. Attorneys may use retainer fees as a down payment on services and, once those fees are exhausted, continue to bill at applicable rates. In contrast, concierge medicine retainer fees are fixed over the designated period. For those concierge models in which the bulk of income resides in this fee (rather than in billing for individual clinical services), the physician's incentive to perform additional, unnecessary services is reduced.

Traditional Payment Systems

Fee-for-Service

Traditionally in this country, physicians have been paid per visit or procedure. This is called *fee-for-service.* The more you do, the more you get paid. You spend time with the patient in the office, you get paid. Spend extra time or with extra complexity, you get paid more. Higher reimbursements are typically allocated for procedures. For example, treating a strained knee with anti-inflammatory medication earns a payment. Injecting a knee with medication earns a higher payment. If surgery is performed on the knee, the payment is higher still. The incentive to do more is clear. In a traditional fee-for-service practice, physicians are even paid for complications, misdiagnoses, or repeat visits for the same problem.

Capitation

Capitation, popularized in the 1990s, is coming back into vogue. This involves physicians and hospitals assuming risk for certain aspects of patient care by accepting fixed payments at a yearly rate. If the cost of care for a group of patients in any given year is less than negotiated, the providers divide up the savings. Alternatively, if the costs exceed the negotiated rate, the providers have less money to share. The incentive is to deliver care that is less costly. A criticism of this model is that it leads to temptation to withhold necessary care.

Pay for Value

Another model of payment ties outcomes to reimbursements. It seems fair to reward physicians and hospitals when they perform better service at a lower cost. However, in most instances today, if costs are reduced, the benefit accrues to the payer, usually the insurance company. For example, a physician who works hard to control diabetes or high blood pressure is likely to have patients with fewer complications from these chronic conditions. This saves the payer from having to pay the hospital and the physician from having to treat diabetic complications. Financially, the payer benefits. In contrast, in the fee-for-service arrangement, a patient who requires treatment again for the same problem disadvantages the payer, but the provider gets paid more. New models are attempting to more properly align incentives. The best-known examples of such outcomes-based payments are the Medicare Hospital Readmissions Reduction Program (Centers for Medicare and Medicaid Services, 2017e) and the Hospital Value-Based Purchasing Program (Centers for Medicare and Medicaid Services, 2017c).

Under the Hospital Value-Based Purchasing Program, Medicare awards hospitals incentive payments or penalties based on the quality of care they provide. This is determined using measures included in the "Total Performance Score," which covers clinical care (evidence-based process and 30-day mortality measures), patient- and caregiver-centered care, safety, and efficiency/cost reduction (Centers for Medicare and Medicaid Services, 2017b). The program is funded by with-holding 2% of participating hospitals' Medicare payments during the fiscal year, and then redistributing the pool of funds according to hospitals' performance. The redistributed payments that hospitals earn depend on the range and distribution of all eligible/participating hospitals' Total Performance Scores, but a hospital can earn, or lose, as much as 2% of its payments for the entire fiscal year.

The Hospital Readmissions Reduction Program functions differently, involving only penalties—up to a 3% reduction of a hospital's base operating Medicare payments—for hospitals with "excess" 30-day readmissions for a chosen set of diagnoses. For fiscal year 2017, these diagnoses include acute myocardial infarction, heart failure, pneumonia, chronic obstructive pulmonary disease, hip/knee replacement, and coronary artery bypass surgery (Centers for Medicare and Medicaid Services, 2017e).

The penalties and incentives under these models are clear: Medicare patients who go home after treatment for the target conditions (e.g., heart failure) and then fail to comply with the prescribed medication regimens or dietary plans (e.g., a low-sodium diet for heart failure) become a problem for hospitals. A readmission to the hospital may not garner sufficient compensation to cover overhead costs.

Bundled Payments

Another "pay-for-value" approach, with which both Medicare and commercial insurance companies are experimenting, uses bundled payments rather than explicit incentives or penalties. In these payment arrangements, the reimbursement for an entire episode of care—such as a total knee replacement or a coronary artery bypass operation—bundles together the payments for the hospital, all the physicians, any post-acute care required (e.g., skilled nursing home facility, cardiac rehabilitation program), and any follow-up care required during a defined post-discharge period. The bundled payment is fixed and unwavering, regardless of what complications arise or the total time for which the patient requires hospitalization. If the cost to the physicians and hospitals is less than the payment, they get to divide up the difference. If the costs are higher, they likewise share the loss in an agreed-upon manner. Similar to capitation, the intent of bundled payments is to reward lower cost of care—but by relying on per episode of care rather than per-patient payments (Centers for Medicare and Medicaid Services, 2017b).

Examples of payment models are summarized in Table 1.1.

Table 1.1   Payment Models

	Fee-for-Service	*Capitation*	*Bundled Payments*
Features	Payment is provided for each visit or procedure	A health care provider is paid a fixed amount per patient during a given period of time	Providers are paid on the basis of expected costs for clinically defined episodes of care
Advantages	May motivate providers to be more productive than under salaried arrangements	Lowers the risk of patients being overtreated and provides more predictable income for physicians	Discourages unnecessary or redundant care and encourages care coordination across providers
Disadvantages	Provides incentive for physicians to provide more treatments because payment is dependent on the quantity rather than quality of care	Physicians need to keep costs down to earn incentives, which may diminish care access and quality, especially for patients with complex conditions	May encourage providers to avoid patients with higher risk factors for whom reimbursement may be inadequate

Financial Structures and Legal Issues for Concierge Medicine

Concierge medicine's retainer fees can be structured under two different scenarios (Table 1.2). In one model, the retainer fee covers certain amenities—such as 24/7 access to the physician,

Table 1.2   Retainer Fee Models

Model	Billing	Included Services	Advantages	Challenges
Retainer fee with insurance billing	Bills insurance companies and health plans for routine services	24/7 access, same-day appointments, extended visits	Billing is performed in a traditional fashion, and patient can utilize health insurance	Retainer fees cannot be attributed to contracted services (i.e., no "double dipping")
Retainer fee with no insurance billing	Bills patients directly	All services (excluding hospital, specialty, and certain outpatient services)	Simplicity of billing	Less affordable for some patients

same-day appointments, and extended focused visits—but does not cover clinical services. With this option, the practice continues to bill insurance companies and government health plans for office visits, laboratory studies, radiology studies, and hospital visits, exactly as is done in traditional fee-for-service medical practices. Under this structure, it is critical that retainer fees do not cover services that are reimbursable by the patient's payer, and marketing and contracting materials should be clear on this issue. Receiving a retainer fee that covers services reimbursable by the payer and billing the payer for such services as well would be considered double dipping and is prohibited by Medicare, Medicaid, and most insurance companies.

In another model, the concierge medicine retainer fee covers all services with the concierge physician and his or her staff, *including* office visits, laboratory studies, some radiology procedures, and selected medications. Specialty visits, hospital charges, and selected outpatient services are typically *excluded*. Retainer fees in this model tend to be higher.

Challenges with this method are risks of running afoul of state insurance laws: in some states, prepayment for services in the absence of appropriate insurance licensure is prohibited, as it may be interpreted as mimicking an insurance premium or capitation payment.

Physicians should seek guidance from legal experts in addressing these administrative and regulatory issues before entering the practice of concierge medicine (Portman and Romanow, 2008).

Who Enrolls in Concierge Medicine?

Many people join a concierge model because of long-standing relationships with a physician. As one senior physician once explained, "After 40 years, I don't have anyone that I simply consider a patient: they are all personal friends." While such a close, satisfying relationship is influential when patients are considering following their physician into a retainer-fee con-cierge model, it is not always determinative. Physicians who have made the transition to the concierge model report that the patients who signed up for the new model were invari-ably *not* always the ones that they expected. On one hand, some patients simply cannot afford the added expense of the retainer fee. Others may have available funds, but cannot justify it to themselves—they see greater value in using those funds elsewhere. A past patient of mine expressed another viewpoint: "I have paid into Medicare throughout my working life; it should now cover my medical expenses."

On the other hand, some patients with lesser financial resources greatly value the physician relationship and strain their budgets to afford the additional cost of the retainer fee. As an example, one of the first patients to join my concierge practice was a retired lower-income worker whom I had not expected to follow me through the transition. In fact, when he received my announcement in the mail, he drove an hour through a thunderstorm to sign up. As he smacked his signed contract on my receptionist's desk, he announced, "You can't leave me, doc. I depend on you."

So, what attracts patients to concierge medicine? The motivations are multiple and can include improved access, extra attention, more face time, or the continuation of a valued relationship. Patient attributes that make them more likely to value and/or benefit from the concierge model include chronic or multiple medical conditions, and busy lifestyles that make the convenience and flexibility appealing. Because concierge practices require an extra expense, the rationale for joining involves a financial consideration. The funding source, however, is not always from the patients themselves.

WHO PAYS FOR CONCIERGE MEDICINE:
1. The patient
2. Spouse of the patient
3. Adult children of the patient
4. Parents of children who value extra attention for their offspring
5. Companies with benefits that cover the concierge fee

Many concierge practices have "scholarship" programs that allow low-income patients to be enrolled without paying the retainer fee. My own concierge practice, Signature Medicine, has such a program—encouraged by Baylor Scott & White Health as aligning with its organizational mission:

> Baylor Scott & White Health exists to serve all people by providing personalized health and wellness through exemplary care, education and research as a Christian ministry of healing.

Thus, when patients have incomes below the federal poverty level, they are accepted as non-paying members with Signature Medicine. We bill insurance, Medicare, or Medicaid, if available, but forego the retainer fee.

Some of these patients have Medicaid coverage and have been treated by me for many years: they qualified as non-paying participants and followed me into my concierge practice. Another group joined initially as paying clients, then fell on hard times and met the requirements for our scholarship program. Two of these patients have since gotten "back into the chips" and returned to full paying status.

One unforgettable and delightful scholarship patient, EH, has followed me since my days as an intern. I cared for her during my training and remember vividly the challenge of a pregnancy due to her sickle cell disease. I helped to manage her pregnancy and the delivery of a healthy baby boy, and we formed a lasting friendship. When I finished my residency, she followed me into private practice, and again followed me when I started my concierge practice. EH has a direct, outspoken style that led to one particularly memorable incident.

My wife is a registered nurse and often fills in when my regular nurse is out. EH was scheduled to be my first patient on one such day. She arrived a bit early and immediately asked why my nurse was not present. I explained that my regular nurse was off but I had a backup who would join us shortly. Ten minutes later, when my wife walked in, EH challenged her, saying, "Dr. Winter's nurse is never late for Dr. Winter." My wife bristled, and, to be truthful, I had fun egging EH on. After a few more criticisms directed at my wife, EH announced that the problem with my "substitute nurse" was that she was too "UPPITY." I figured that my wife had had enough so I exposed our relationship. We all had a good laugh (at least EH and I did), and, to this day, EH continues to ask how my uppity nurse/wife is doing.

What Is Included in a Concierge Service?

Typical expectations from concierge patients are immediate access, unrushed office visits, 24/7 availability (phone, e-mail, texting, videoconference), and an exceptional service experience. House calls, hospital visits, and accompanying patients to specialist appointments are often included. Additional services from contracted dieticians, exercise physiologists, and trainers may be offered. Genetic screening, exercise stress tests, body mass index testing, computed tomography (CT) body scans, visual exams, and hearing tests may also be available through concierge practices. One of the greatest benefits, however, is the establishment and maintenance of a physician–patient relationship that enables the physician to interpret the patient's symptoms in the full light of that patient's history and personality. For example, one of my patients, an athletic middle-aged man, came in one day complaining of back pain after a competitive basketball game with his buddies. I knew JW well and, although he described the game as combative, I knew he had played similarly strenuous games for years, is quite stoic, and had never required treatment for injuries sustained on the basketball court. He insisted that his symptoms were purely the result of his on-court exertions, but I suspected there was more to the story. Scans of his back, which he initially refused but on which I eventually prevailed, revealed a rare form of bone cancer. Knowing the individual gives a huge advantage to the physician—and, therefore, to the patient.

Beyond the routine preventive medicine, screening, and disease management that fill much of any primary care physician's day, travel medicine advice is a common aspect of working with concierge patients. As more patients travel, they often anticipate medical illnesses and conditions that can occur far away from contact with their physician. In addition, many foreign countries require documentation of immunizations prior to entry. Malaria and hepatitis prevention are important in certain areas. West Nile virus, dengue fever, and the Zika virus are of more concern recently. I favor a "travel package" including medications for allergies, diarrhea, tropical illnesses, motion sickness, and infections, depending upon the areas to be visited. Many of these medications can be purchased without a prescription. It is useful to go over the circumstances in which they should be taken. And, of course, the 24/7 availability via phone, e-mail, or other telecommunications remains in place while patients travel. Some concierge practices—those with very small panel sizes and concomitantly higher retainer fees— even extend travel packages to the point of traveling with their patients (or, at least, visiting them in a foreign city or country when requested).

The words "house call" evoke images of the bygone horse-and-buggy days, when country doctors traveled to visit patients in their homes, carrying the ubiquitous black bag, and payment could be bartered with eggs, chickens, or pigs (Figure 1.1).

Figure 1.1 Everything old becomes new again. (From http://www.skok-iehistory.org/gallery/people1800f/people1800s.htm.)

While house calls are seeing a resurgence in modern medicine—especially in the concierge medicine model—eggs, chickens, and pigs are not usually accepted as payment.

House calls are certainly not the most efficient use of a physician's time, but patients thrill at having the doctor come to them, making this a fairly common service to be included in concierge medicine. They also have advantages for the physician. The relaxed setting of a patient's home often provides valuable insight into the health and care of a patient. I once made a house call to a patient with recurrent congestive heart failure. Since my visit coincided with his lunch time, he and his wife invited me to share in their meal: sandwiches and potato chips. I became alarmed when my patient began eating salty chips, and I launched into a discussion about how salt adds to fluid retention, shortness of breath, and hospital admissions for patients with heart failure. The patient rebutted that he was aware that salt should be restricted, and that he only ate low-salt chips. I leaned over, grabbed one of his chips, and was not surprised by the briny taste. It was definitely not low in salt. We had a long talk about how salt affects a weak heart and the benefits of a low-salt diet (which would exclude potato chips). The patient learned a valuable lesson, avoided chips thereafter, and had no further exacerbations of his congestive heart failure.

Executive physical programs are also often tied to concierge models. These programs typically include extensive evaluations with lots of "bells and whistles" and have been criticized for performing unnecessary and duplicative tests. These tests increase costs, and can lead to unnecessary anxiety and further testing when false positives or ambiguous results return (Komaroff, 2009). A bigger concern is that companies that conduct executive physicals "in house" separate patients from their personal physician during the kind of visit that allows for patients and physicians to best get to know each other. This is an ideal time to conduct a thorough review of a patient's concerns, history, symptoms, family history, stressors, eating patterns, and exercise habits. It is during these encounters that the patient and physician also build mutual trust and an understanding of each other's personalities and tendencies. By moving executive physicals into a concierge practice, the corporate program ties the annual physical to a physician who, with added insight, can better attend to the patient's needs throughout the year. This has the added advantage of helping patients to avoid unnecessary, duplicative testing that can occur when they visit separate providers and facilities. Busy executives also often enjoy the benefit of a concierge relationship with its 24/7 access and prompt response to medical issues (Signature MD, 2017).

Set up properly, a concierge medicine practice can ensure that there is always time and room for the patient to call, pop in, or e-mail a concern and receive unhurried, focused attention to their needs. If you have an eight o'clock appointment, you will be seen at eight o'clock. No more need to bring a book or a computer to occupy your time while you wait to be seen. The concept of a waiting room thus becomes obsolete. There may be a "greeting room" where patients are welcomed by name and offered a cool beverage or coffee. In addition to such staff-provided hospitality, my patients often enjoy running into other patients with whom they are familiar, and the greeting room provides a pleasant environment in which they can do so.

Running on time is a luxury for both the patient and the physician. Visits in a concierge medicine practice are unhurried, and detailed discussions on a variety of issues are possible. There is always time to administer or schedule any immunizations or preventive studies that are due, and to review previous studies, consultations, emergency visits, and hospital stays.

Another benefit to the unhurried nature of the concierge medicine office visit is that notes are thorough and can be shared with the patient during the visit, and copies can later be mailed or accessed via computer. Such sharing helps to clarify patients' understanding and reinforces instructions. Additionally, the patient has the opportunity to offer edits or additions when appropriate, which not only improves communication but enhances trust in the relationship. While patient access to their own charts—and even the ability to add information to them—is becoming more common in traditional medical practices with the advent of electronic health records and patient portals, time restrictions on office visits in traditional settings seldom accommodate such collaborative reviews of the chart.

Another advantage of concierge medicine is the time and attention to the patients and their issues, even when they are not in the office. This gives the physician time and opportunity to think about, follow up with, and problem-solve the issues discussed during the visit. A busy non-concierge physician with a large panel of patients may adroitly care for each when sitting in front of the patient in the exam room, but, once the patient leaves, the physician must quickly change focus to the next patient. There is little time for reflection or to mull over details of a patient visit. Many physicians, myself included, have had experiences in which we solve complicated medical issues while driving or during other uninterrupted times. The pace of concierge practices allows more of those opportunities.

The process of referral to specialists is similar in concierge medicine to that in traditional practices. The concierge physician or staff recommends a referral, sends records in advance, and provides contact information for the chosen specialist. When urgent, a phone call from the physician directly to the specialist may hasten the appointment date. Concierge physicians cannot necessarily obtain specialty appointments any faster than physicians in traditional practices. Referral access correlates with relationships that a physician has cultivated with the specialists. It has been suggested that concierge practices should consider sharing a portion of the retainer fee with specialists to provide faster referral access, but this is not a good idea. Both state and federal laws are strict about payments to induce or reward referrals, and they carry weighty penalties when violated.

Concierge patients may experience a nice opportunity with regard to specialty referrals: the opportunity to have their doctor accompany them to specialist appointments. This is difficult for physicians in traditional practices, for whom such an activity would represent both lost revenue and lost appointment times for other patients. Concierge physicians can more readily accommodate such services in their schedules, greatly improving the coordination of care for complex patients.

As an example, one of my patients, diagnosed with liver cancer, was struggling with a major decision regarding his treatment options. Our studies showed that his cancer was confined to his liver, and liver transplantation was being considered. However, his tumor volume was greater than accepted by the United Network of Organ Sharing, which sets standards for who can and cannot receive a donated organ. The oncologist had proposed chemotherapy in an attempt to shrink the tumors to meet transplant guidelines, but that did not sound promising. My patient was perplexed and frustrated, so I offered to go with him on his next consultation.

I contacted the specialist first and got his blessing to attend the scheduled appointment. The issue for the patient was not being eligible for a liver transplant. He inquired about transplant options overseas. The specialist agreed that a transplant could be bought in some countries. I had remained quiet but at that point spoke up, asking where the donors came from. The specialist answered that a young healthy patient would receive a bullet to the head, and the family would be paid a nominal sum for the sacrifice. My patient shuddered and later told me that my question was the one that he did not know to ask, but was pivotal for his decision. He gave up his quest for a transplant.

Chapter 2

What Do Concierge Medicine Practices Look Like?

Prices for and services offered by concierge practices vary widely. Practices at the high end of the market, such as Private Medical group out of San Francisco and Seattle's MD², may have retainer fees from $20,000 up to $80,000 per patient per year (MD², 2017; MacDonald, 2017; Schwartz, 2017). In this model, physicians typically cap their practices at fewer than 100 patients per physician. In addition to unhurried visits and prompt access, these physicians offer extra services, such as traveling with their patients. The market for this high-end model is demonstrated by the spread of these models in large cities across eight different states (MacDonald, 2017; Long, 2016).

MDVIP is another national concierge network, more moderately priced at $1,500–$1,800 per patient per year, with each physician's panel size running up to 600 patients. This organization reports 800 physicians in 42 states and markets a concept of freedom (MDVIP marketing brochure, 2017):

Freedom to practice medicine the way you aspire to
Freedom to enjoy the people and activities that bring balance to your life
Freedom to earn the financial security you desire
Freedom to have control over your life—professionally, personally, and financially

Health care systems such as Virginia Mason Medical System in Seattle, Scripps Health in San Diego, and University of California San Diego Health sponsor their own concierge practices (Scripps, 2017; UC San Diego Health, 2017; Virginia Mason, 2017). Paladina Health in Denver reports physician patient panel sizes 70% lower than those of traditional primary care practices to facilitate easy access and longer appointments (*Sealover*, 2012). Some, such as Lux Health Network in Beverly Hills, California, go beyond primary care to offer specialty concierge practices.

Unlike these prominent examples, the majority of concierge practices "fly under the radar" and exist independently without direct ties to hospital systems or networks of physicians. Such practices are facing challenges with the proliferation of narrow network health plans, in which patients have substantial financial incentives to seek care only through affiliated physicians and hospitals. (The incentives include high deductibles that the patient must pay before the insurance plan pays, and co-pays or upfront payments for each service and visit.) The American Society for Concierge Physicians was founded in 2003 to represent these independent concierge practices (American Academy of Private Physicians, 2017).

Chapter 3

Other Concierge Models

The previous section explained full-scale concierge practices, but there are other models. Addressing the impatience that many people increasingly seem to have when they are ill or injured, what can be called "concierge lite" models have emerged. These are well-organized groups of physicians, along with advanced practitioners and nurses or medical assistants, who collectively care for panels of patients. The patients identify with the clinic, rather than with one individual physician. A linked computer system allows clinicians to access the patient's data at any clinic location or via a smartphone or tablet. Multiple clinic sites provide patients with the convenience of different locations, near either their homes or their offices, in addition to remote 24/7 access to the on-call provider via e-mail, telephone, text, or videoconference.

Tele-visits, which enable face-to-face discussions via smartphone or webcam, are increasingly being offered by commercial telemedicine companies, as well as precocious health care systems. Both full concierge and "concierge lite" practices have been quick to adopt this technical advantage (Terry, 2015).

The use of e-mail for patient communication is not unique to concierge models. Providers in some standard primary care practices are extending their personal e-mail addresses to selected patients. This may or may not come with a cost to the patient. On one hand, most physicians give advice over the *telephone* to their patients at no additional charge. Free advice over the Internet, on the other hand, is a nice service for patients but adds time to already-beleaguered physicians' schedules. For traditional physician practices with large patient panels, such e-mail access can be overwhelming. One physician of my acquaintance reported returning from a two-week vacation to find more than 400 e-mails from her patients. Similarly, over weekends when a single physician is on call for his or her partners in traditional practices, that physician is "contactable" by upwards of 10,000 patients (assuming an average practice size of five physicians, each with an average panel size of 2,000 patients). Because of the overwhelming numbers and busy schedules that typify traditional primary care practice models, patient e-mails can become more of a burden than a helpful communication tool. In contrast, the concierge medicine setting with smaller panel sizes enables physicians and practice staff to keep abreast of daily inquiries without being overwhelmed. Concierge physicians are usually more accessible (most or all of the time), but the numbers of calls or e-mails are fewer, corresponding with the smaller panel size. Another advantage of smaller panel sizes is that the physician is more familiar with each patient. Familiarity with patients streamlines medical decision making.

While concierge medicine has existed largely in the primary care domain to date, some specialty physicians are establishing retainer fee models for chronic diseases, such as cardiologists for congestive heart failure and endocrinologists for juvenile onset diabetes mellitus. Such programs may facilitate superior control of that individual condition, but run the risk of inadvertently focusing on one aspect of a patient's health to the exclusion of others. Juvenile diabetics, for example, are not immune from appendicitis, and heart-failure patients can also come down with infections and cancer. As a consequence, these specialty concierge services need to include close collaboration with their patients' primary care physicians to ensure that comprehensive care is provided.

Another model for health care delivery is the employer clinic, set up to allow prompt access for employees. The idea is to get employees seen quickly and minimize time away from work. These clinics are frequently staffed by advanced practice providers (nurse practitioners or physician assistants) and supervised by physicians, but may also be staffed by physicians themselves. They are typically located on the employer's campus or in close proximity.

I fully expect other models to appear, along with combinations and hybrids of today's models. As mentioned previously, the U.S. health care system is ripe for disruption. While this derives from the significant challenges in meeting our patients' and population's health needs with existing resources and structures, it also provides an environment in which entrepreneurial ingenuity can be inspired by those unmet needs.

Where Did Concierge Medicine Come From?

Why did the concierge model of medicine arise? Concierge medicine is being driven by both physicians and patients: patients are becoming less satisfied with current health care delivery, and physicians are increasingly frustrated with their workload.

Patient Frustrations

> A familiar physician can play such a vital role in improving and maintaining your health.
>
> **Peter Anderson, MD and Paul Grundy, MD**
> *(Anderson, 2014)*

On one hand, more than 90% of patients are satisfied with their relationship with their primary care doctor, according to a survey conducted on behalf of the Physicians Foundation

(The Physicians Foundation, 2016). They feel that their doctors are respectful of them, listen well, and explain well. On the other hand, they are *not* happy with the administrative aspects of medicine—making appointments, scheduling procedures, paying bills, dealing with insurance companies … the "hassles."

Office schedules tend to revolve around the physician and not the patients. Most clinics still do not have extended operating hours or weekend availability. When patients arrive at the clinic, front office employees often curtly ask them to repeat their insurance verification and then "take a seat." Not always the best first impression.

Making appointments can be a struggle. Sick patients often need attention that is not delayed or difficult to schedule. One of my partners received this letter from a patient:

> Dr. _____,
> My name is _____. My husband and I are longtime (probably 15 years) patients of Dr. _____, MD. In this letter I would like to address issues I have had with the appointment scheduling in the last two weeks and also, in the past. Coming off a cruise on February 26, I became sick with fever, nausea, and congestion on February 28; and my illness progressed. On March 1, I went to an urgent care facility where I was diagnosed with an upper respiratory infection and prescribed Azithromycin. Around 11 p.m. on March 2, I went to an emergency room with breathing problems. Both facilities did blood work, chest x-rays, etc., and told me to follow up with my regular doctor within seven days. I called Dr. _____ office on March 3 and tried to schedule an appointment with an appointment scheduler. She said Dr. _____ didn't have an opening until March 29 and that they were overrun with sick people. I asked to speak with Dr. _____'s nurse; the scheduler refused to let me speak with her. I asked to leave a

message with the nurse saying that I was sick, and
she had been very good at working me in when I
am sick. He refused to let me leave a message. He
offered for me to see a nurse practitioner; I emphati-
cally refused that offer. Then, he said he could put
me on a cancellation list which I agreed to; but of
course, that phone call never came. In the mean-
time, my illness progressed and on March 4 around
midnight, I went back to the emergency department.
I was diagnosed with double ear infections on top
of everything else. Again, blood work, chest x-rays,
etc. were taken; and I was prescribed Augmentin
and Promethazine for nausea. I was told to follow up
with my regular doctor within seven days—no luck
there. I was very sick by March 8, so my daughter
took me to a different emergency department. There,
I was diagnosed with double pneumonia and was
hospitalized for three days. In conjunction with all of
my medical issues, I ran a fever with nausea for 10
days. Before I was released from the hospital a case
worker met with me and told me to follow up with
my regular doctor within seven days. I told him my
story with my doctor's office and of my inability to
get an appointment. He said that was unacceptable
and that he would call and get me an appointment
with my doctor. After playing phone tag all afternoon, he had to leave a message for a return call to
me with an appointment with Dr. _____. When the
appointment scheduler finally called me, she said Dr. ____
had *no* availability. I reminded her of the phone call
from the case worker, and he said, "How many days
did he say?" I told her seven, she said just a minute
and came back with an appointment at 1 p.m. on
March 16.

This appointment/message problem with the
schedulers at _____clinic has been ongoing. My

husband and I discussed this issue with Dr. _____ at our annual physicals in December. He is very displeased with the system and has tried to address the problem in physicians' meetings, etc.; but evidently, it has fallen on deaf ears. Dr. _____ and _____ are wonderful medical professionals and are *not* part of this problem in any way. We love having Dr._____ and _____as our health care providers.

Follow-up letter:

This issue has just escalated out of control! I just received a call from _____ saying that I would need to reschedule my appointment to next Thursday, March 23, as Dr. _____ is *not* going to be in the office this afternoon. I told her this is not acceptable. She came back with an 8 a.m. appointment tomorrow morning, March 17. We will do our best to make the appointment, but this is a real hardship for us as we live on the edge of McKinney. We will have to leave home at 6:30 a.m. and fight the Friday rush-hour traffic all the way to downtown Dallas. According to the case worker, this scheduling problem and my *inability* to get an appointment with my doctor is a totally unacceptable practice. Please help me get this problem rectified!!!

My care at _____ and with Dr. _____ was *superb* in every way! I feel that it shortened my recovery by several weeks. But, had I been able to get in to see Dr. _____, I believe he could have saved me from the many ER visits and possibly hospitalization.

Please let me know how this situation will be corrected, so patients and doctors/nurses can have an open line of communication and patients can get the help they need from their doctor in a timely manner.

Unfortunately, obtaining prompt appointments for medical problems is becoming more of a challenge in this country.
Shortages of primary care physicians and selected specialists
exacerbate the issue. Just attempting to schedule an appointment in a physician's office can be maddening:

> (Recorded message) *"Hello, thank you for calling the _____*
> *clinic.*
> *If this is an emergency, hang up and dial 911.*
> *If this is a doctor's office and you want to speak to the*
> *doctor, press 1.*
> *If this is a doctor's office and you do not need to speak*
> *to the doctor but have other questions, press 2.*
> *If you would like to speak to the nurse, press 3.*
> *If you would like directions on how to get to our*
> *clinic, press 4.*
> *If you are a patient and have questions about billing,*
> *press 5.*
> *If you are a patient and would like to schedule an*
> *appointment, press 6.*
> *If you would like to leave a message, press 7.*
> *If you would like to repeat this message, press 8."*

And how about visiting a physician's office? Are the clinics, or for that matter the hospitals, designed for patients, or
for physicians? One indication is found in the parking lots.
The closest parking spots often say, "Physician Parking Only"
(Figure 3.1).

From the patient perspective, there are a myriad of issues
with the current system. Understandably, when patients have a
medical issue, serious or not, they want to visit, or at least talk
to, their doctor. They also crave and deserve a physician who
is attentive and unrushed. That need was more often fulfilled
in the past. What has happened?

Where is the idealized Dr. Marcus Welby? In the 1960s and
1970s, Robert Young portrayed a family physician on television

Figure 3.1 "Physician Parking Only" sign. (From trgowanlock - stock. adobe.com.)

who exuded compassion and gave unlimited attention to each patient, often in the patient's home. His knowledge was unlimited and his bedside manner impeccable. This exaggerated portrayal made for good television, but also set unrealistic expectations. It should also be pointed out that health care in this country has changed.

One important change relates to reimbursements. These have steadily declined for most physicians and, to compensate, many have tried to squeeze more visits and more procedures into each day (Matthews, 2015). More visits crammed into the work day can squeeze out time for relaxed, detailed discussions. Some physicians have given up trying. They are referred to as "doorway doctors," a name that emphasizes their tendency to stand in exam room or hospital doorways, ask a few quick questions, and then leave before the patient has much time to reply.

Another important change is the practice of medicine itself (Table 3.1). Many years ago, medicine was less complicated and less rushed. It was also a lot less effective. We now have

Table 3.1 Medical Practice 100 Years Ago and Today

Medical Practice 100 Years Ago	Medical Practice Today
Simple	Complicated
Not very effective	Highly effective
Safe	Risky
Inexpensive	Expensive
Satisfying to patients and physicians	Variable

amazing treatments including powerful antibiotics, techniques to reverse strokes and heart attacks, and even cures for some cancers. The proliferation of knowledge has, in turn, led to greater specialization within medicine—an orthopedic friend of mine half-jokingly says that he is so specialized that he only does knee arthroscopies and now wants to restrict these to only right knees.

Specialization improves outcomes. For example, heart surgery programs that perform more than 250 coronary bypass operations annually have better outcomes than those that perform fewer (Hornik et al., 2012). Complex procedures such as Whipple operations for pancreatic cancers and esophagus resections for tumors also have better outcomes at centers with higher volumes (Birkmeyer et al., 1999; Dimick et al., 2003).

Focusing on a narrow field may enable a physician to develop greater expertise or skills, but it also complicates the patient's job of accessing the proper provider to address his or her concerns. In addition, some highly skilled specialists are uncomfortable outside their area of expertise and give less attention to the total care of the patient. So, while our operations, treatments, and diagnostics have improved considerably over time, the *care* of patients sometimes gets lost in the system. Patients' complaints frequently deal with lack of consistency, poor coordination, safety issues, and poor communication. We are challenged to put all the knowledge, all the skills, and all the courtesies of attentive service together at every contact.

An additional challenge lies in the fact that we live in a world in which the answer to every question is seemingly only a mouse click away. Many answers can indeed be obtained via online search engines. Many incorrect and misleading answers can also be obtained in this way.

Physician Frustrations

> In the current environment of time-pressured primary care, it's hard to envision having sufficient opportunity during a periodic health exam for the type of in-depth, personalized conversation necessary to create and sustain a meaningful doctor–patient relationship.
>
> **Allan H. Goroll, MD** *(Goroll, 2015)*

The "hamster wheel" schedules that have evolved in the fee-for-service setting are *not* working for an increasing percentage of physicians. Many report frustration and even frank burnout (Shanafelt and Noseworthy, 2017). An increasing number of comments refer to "losing the joy of medicine." A slower pace with more time to visit with patients can be a prime motive for those switching to concierge practices—especially when there is the potential for seeing fewer patients without having to take a cut in pay. Others mention protocol-driven mandates as the source of their dissatisfaction. Concierge physicians in large medical groups are not immune from committee-driven policies and protocols, but may be less susceptible to the frustration of having "one more thing on their plate." Physicians nearing retirement also may feel inadequate or just plain fatigued at the intensity of their work (Figure 3.2).

Figure 3.2 Physician frustrations. (From kite_rin - stock.adobe.com.)

The issues contributing to physicians' frustration can be summarized as the Six Cs:

Computers
Coding
Compliance
Costs
Consumerism
Criteria

Of all the contributors to the unhappiness of providers (physicians, nurses, physician assistants, and nurse practitioners), *computers* top the list. Computers have shoehorned themselves into the day-to-day work of physicians. Through federal government incentives, they have become the necessary manner in which physicians record what they do. The 2009 Health Information Technology for Economic and Clinical Health (HITECH) Act pushed many physicians into the computer age through a program called Meaningful Use

(HealthIT.gov, 2017). This is a Medicare and Medicaid program that provides incentives for using certified electronic health record software for specified aspects of patient care and communication. The intent of the program was to promote the widespread use of documentation in electronic health records.

> It's what's right for the patient, and our goal as a country to get to better health, better health care and lower costs.
>
> **Farzad Mostashari, MD** *(AthenaHealth, 2017)*
> *Former National Coordinator for Health*
> *Information Technology*
> *U.S. Department of Health and Human Services*

Electronic medical records certainly have some advantages. The problem for physicians lies in the fact that they are often required to spend more time on the computer and more time away from patients. Many providers report spending several hours at the end of each day banging away on computer keyboards. Patients complain about a lack of eye contact during office visits as physicians appear to spend more time looking at their monitors than at the patients themselves.

The Meaningful Use program requires documentation that does not always appear to add to patient care. Sometimes double or even triple documentation is required. It also forces physicians to change their work flows; for many, these are habits that have accumulated over a number of years. Frustrations with this have led some physicians to nickname the program "Meaning*less* Use."

On the other hand, computers are transforming health care delivery in positive ways. They allow us to better keep track of our patients and their needs. They allow us to compile data and to analyze it for research and improvement projects. They have eliminated errors related to physicians' handwriting—although they have introduced their own risks related to issues such as look-alike, sound-alike drug names in selection lists.

On the positive side, they also facilitate rapid communication between patients and physicians, and among physicians themselves. Redundant duplication of imaging and laboratory tests occurs less frequently in the context of electronic health records since, to the extent that interoperability exists between computer systems, they enable the physician to see all of a patient's recent or past test results. Additionally, the volume of new medical information that is accumulating makes computer-assisted decision making not only plausible but an important asset in clinical practice. It is estimated that from 2020 on, the amount of medical information produced every year will double (Densen, 2011). Physicians just cannot keep up with the evolving science of medicine without computer support.

Coding is another unwelcome challenge and a frequent omission in the education of young physicians. The federal government has led the way in the development of complicated coding schemes to track the work of physicians. While the underlying motive is to control costs, the current International Classification of Disease (ICD-10) coding compendium contains 14,000 separate items that try to define the work of physicians down to minute detail. It is easy to make fun of the unlikely situations that are included in this latest edition:

V97.33XD. Sucked into jet engine, subsequent encounter
Z63.1. Problems in relationship with in-laws
W22.02XD. Spacecraft collision injuring occupant, sequela
W55.22XA. Struck by a turtle
W61.33XA. Pecked by chicken, initial encounter
V91.07XA. Burn due to water-ski on fire, initial encounter

However, this light relief fades in the frustration of trying to pick the relevant code for a seemingly simple diagnosis. Take, for example, bronchitis. Which of the following options should a physician pick? Should the physician hire a Master Coder to help choose the right code?

Bronchitis
Tracheobronchitis
Acute bronchitis and bronchiectasis
    Acute bronchitis and chronic obstructive asthma
    Acute bronchitis and chronic obstructive pulmonary
        disease
    Allergic bronchitis
    Bronchitis due to chemicals, fumes and vapors
    Chronic bronchitis
    Chronic mucopurulent bronchitis
    Chronic obstructive bronchitis
    Chronic obstructive tracheobronchitis
    Chronic simple bronchitis
    Chronic tracheobronchitis
    Acute and subacute bronchitis with bronchospasm
    Acute and subacute bronchitis with tracheitis
    Acute and subacute bronchitis with tracheobronchitis,
        acute
    Acute and subacute fibrinous bronchitis
    Acute and subacute membranous bronchitis
    Acute and subacute purulent bronchitis
    Acute and subacute septic bronchitis
    Acute bronchitis due to *Mycoplasma pneumoniae*
    Acute bronchitis due to *Haemophilus influenzae*
    Acute bronchitis due to *Streptococcus*
    Acute bronchitis due to coxsackievirus
    Acute bronchitis due to parainfluenza virus
    Acute bronchitis due to respiratory syncytial virus
    Acute bronchitis due to rhinovirus
    Acute bronchitis due to echovirus
    Acute bronchitis due to other specified organisms
    Acute bronchitis, unspecified

Compliance is defined by Merriam-Webster as the act or process of complying with a desire, demand, proposal, or regimen (*Merriam-Webster Dictionary*, 2017). Most hospitals and health care systems have compliance departments that rival the size and importance of legal, finance, and marketing departments. There are strict rules and guidelines in the health care industry, the complexity of which requires experts to keep physicians out of trouble. There are even legal and medical licensure issues for those who are non-compliant that threaten to fine, suspend, or revoke their license to practice medicine. A posted picture of a surgeon posing with an anesthetized patient in the background led to sanctions for one unwitting physician, even though the patient was not recognizable. Another example involves a physician who allegedly received excessive meals from a pharmaceutical company. He, in fact, had never eaten any of the meals. Unbeknownst to the doctor, his office staff had ordered and enjoyed the perks.

How about the *cost* of health care? Until recently, physicians had little concern for the cost of tests and treatments that they ordered. Medical school professors have been known to exhort young students to "focus on the care of the patient without regard for anything but that what is most important for their care." With the rising cost of health care in this country, that now includes the price of health care services. The costs of lab tests, imaging studies, and procedures are now more commonly identified to the physician as they are ordered. Physicians are admonished to pay attention to costs and, if one pathway is less expensive, all other things being equal, the cheaper one should be chosen. Accountable care organizations may even award bonuses or assess penalties to physician groups based on their costs, as will, from 2020 on, the Quality Payment Program that is replacing Medicare's Sustainable Growth Rate formula under the Medicare Access and CHIP [Children's Health Insurance Program] Reauthorization Act of 2015 (Centers for Medicare and Medicaid Services, 2017d).

What has been labeled the *consumerism* movement is also adding to the demands and potential frustrations of physicians. Merriam-Webster defines consumerism as "the promotion of the consumer's interests" (*Merriam-Webster Dictionary*, 2017). More and more, patient interests include how quickly and conveniently they can get their health care needs addressed. Making an appointment for a physician office visit is not always easy. Pharmacies, urgent care clinics, grocery stores, and web-based information sites are offering medical services in different environments to meet the demand for easily accessible care. Even Apple, Google, and Amazon are rumored to have plans to enter the health care arena.

Younger generations, in particular, are said to want their health care when they want it, where they want it, and how they want it. Steve Jobs gets credit (or blame) for beginning this trend in 2001. His iPod invention taught younger folks that they could play whatever songs they wanted at any time and at any volume they desired. As these youngsters grow up and require health care, they are simply not inclined to accept regimented, inflexible office schedules. I can imagine them thinking, or even saying out loud, "No, not Tuesday at 10:30 a.m., how about now and how about at my home?" Even people from older generations are starting to prefer easier access. Physicians practicing in traditional fee-for-service models have limited ability to adapt their services to these demands while still receiving adequate reimbursement. The resulting frustration has added "consumerism" to the list of "Cs" motivating the transition to the more flexible concierge models.

The sixth C refers to *criteria* with which physicians are expected to comply. The expectation comes from many directions: the government, commercial insurance companies, medical staff departments of hospitals, and the public. Physician groups themselves add to physicians' workloads and frustrations when they demand quality metrics, patient satisfaction surveys, outcome expectations, and safety standards.

Accountable care organizations are also adding criteria with which physicians are expected to comply. Referred to as ACOs, they are virtual alliances of physicians and hospitals that are asked to become accountable for providing better care, better health, and better value to entire populations of patients, payers, and communities (Couch, 2016)—awarding bonuses and penalties according to performance in these domains. Such accountability requires measurement of performance on a variety of quality and cost measures—which, in turn, adds to physicians' documentation burden, leading some to refer to ACOs as "Another Crazy Obstruction."

Frustrations with the six Cs are present in all physician generations, but younger folks as a whole are said to be more malleable. Dr. Robert M. Wachter is a renowned academic physician, author, and patient advocate. He writes of the burdens of modern medicine and their effects on physicians. In one example, he describes a well-intended conversation with young physicians: "I tried to shake students out of their youthful complacency." He lectured, "You folks need to be prepared for a career that will be massively different from mine. You will be under the relentless pressure to deliver the highest quality, safest, most satisfying care at the lowest possible cost." An insightful younger medical student then asked, "What exactly were YOU trying to do?" (Wachter, 2016).

Resiliency is a term that describes the ability to adapt to and bounce back from the stress. This trait can serve as an antidote for the frustration and burnout among the ranks of physicians in America (Finkelstein, 2017). The concierge model is another option to remedy the stress from the pace of traditional medical practices.

Chapter 4

Lessons from Other Industries

Like other aspects of health care—for example, patient
safety, which has drawn heavily on lessons from the avia-
tion industry—concierge medicine takes, and can continue
to learn, lessons from other industries. Service providers that
strive to be "best in class" in other industries are especially
instructive, as concierge medicine seeks to fill an equivalent
niche within health care. The lessons to be learned from other
industries are particularly applicable in dealing with aspects of
modern society—such as information technology and the consumerism movement—that affected or were adopted by other
industries faster than health care.

Aviation

Airline pilots, similar to physicians, are meticulous in their
approach to their occupation. Pre-flight checklists are focused,
detailed, and mandatory. Pre-operative checklists for physicians are comparable and are now routinely used in our
operating rooms. A point can be made that pilots enjoy

flying airplanes, as physicians enjoy caring for their patients. Neither group of professionals relishes documentation mandates. Physicians often spend several hours in the evenings documenting their work. Pilots, on the other hand, walk out of planes with seemingly little need for additional computer entry to record their work, though there is certainly much documentation required while in flight. There may be lessons for concierge and other medical practices from the airline industry on how to more efficiently document pertinent data in real time.

Banking

> "The only industry more regulated today than banking is health care."

Many other industries have gone through convulsive changes led by information technology. Banks today operate quite differently than they did a decade ago. Electronic data systems enable the collection and processing of large volumes of data in the banking industry, but also carry increased risks related to security, privacy, fraud, and money-laundering issues. Computerized medical records also offer advantages to the health care industry but carry added burdens that are common sources of frustrations for physicians. Concierge models often include the use of electronic health records, but the pace of concierge practice allows more tolerance for the additional time required to interact with the computer.

Similarly, increased regulatory burdens affect both banking and the health care industry. The Patriot Act, Sarbanes–Oxley Act, and Dodd–Frank Act all increased the transparency and accountability expected of banks. They also increased burdens on banks by adding to the complexity and cost of doing business in the United States. Studies have suggested that since passage of the Sarbanes–Oxley Act, for example, more businesses are being registered in foreign countries, and others are being deregistered from America's public exchanges (Piotroski and Srinivasan, 2008). It can be argued that the added load of information technology in health care is another factor pushing physicians to consider such options as early retirement or a change in practice styles that includes a concierge practice.

The banking system was faster than the health care industry to adopt the consumer-oriented services information that technology enables—for example, online banking and virtual check deposits using smartphone cameras. Because banking, like health care, involves a need to protect the privacy and security of an individual's information, it provides a good model for the information sharing and access that patients are now looking for in health care.

The primary difference between the use of information technology for data collection, processing, and sharing in banking versus health care resides in the type of data involved. While a significant portion of banking data is literally dollars and cents, health care data consists of detailed, descriptive clinical data that is far more complex both to capture and to analyze. Unfortunately, the complexity of the data that needs to be entered into information systems makes it harder to delegate data entry to non-physicians in health care than to do the equivalent in banking. The need to have highly trained physicians involved in the documentation slows the process down—and, often, requires physicians to devote hours outside of the office to documentation. Additionally, because of the detailed, descriptive nature of the clinical data being entered, most physicians develop their own unique documentation styles, which may not fit well with the formats dictated by the electronic health records. This can make it difficult to aggregate data across physicians to enable the kinds of analyses required to evaluate the quality and outcomes of care.

Automobiles and Automobile Sales

The automotive industry has gone through significant changes. Personal passenger vehicles are now the biggest high-tech purchase most individuals will ever make. Today's cars contain more computer chips and software than the first rockets that astronauts piloted into space. Higher safety standards and consumer expectations, as well as the emphasis on fuel efficiency and low carbon emissions in recent years, have accelerated the pace of automobile technology development. Half of the gasoline engines sold in 2015 were at least 20% more efficient than those sold in 2009 (Office of Energy Efficiency and Renewable Energy, 2017). Electronics now constitute 25% of a car's value—and that number is expected to be 40% in the next 5–10 years (The Statistics Portal, 2017). While these developments have increased the complexity of cars and raised their sales prices, cars are safer and more reliable than before. These attributes, together with the necessity of individual cars for transportation in cities that lack strong public transportation infrastructure, have led to steady consumer demand for automobiles despite the higher prices—although new car prices are rapidly approaching the tipping point at which they will be unaffordable for the majority of Americans (Carns, 2016).

Health care is in a similar situation: scientific and technological advances have produced a wider range of more effective treatments than was previously available. However, the price of these options and effectiveness is higher costs, a greater workload for providers, and greater complexity for both patients and providers. The health information technology that is becoming so essential to the delivery of that effective care also comes with a hefty price tag: in the millions of dollars for hospitals and up to several hundred dollars per month for physicians.

While the health care industry as a whole can probably learn valuable lessons from the automobile industry regarding the need to balance innovation and advancement against affordability for products and services that are household necessities, concierge medicine has the most to gain from studying the sales and customer service approaches employed by luxury car dealerships. Like concierge medicine, these dealerships are selling something beyond the basic necessity. Their approaches toward convincing customers that the additional benefits they offer are worth higher prices may be instructive.

Carl Sewell, a successful Dallas-based automobile executive whose dealerships largely specialize in luxury brands such as Audi, BMW, Cadillac, and Mercedes-Benz, teaches that everyone in the automobile business sells cars, and they therefore have to compete on the service they deliver.

> "Our only source of competitive advantage is our people and the service they provide."
>
> **Carl Sewell** *(Sewell and Brown, 2002)*

Drive into one of his dealerships and you are instantly addressed by a friendly greeter who gathers your request, triages you to the appropriate service representative, and offers you a snack and a beverage. As a customer of the Sewell dealerships, I have never met one of their mechanics, nor do I need to do so. The service representative gives me the distinct impression that he is my advocate, indeed, my ombudsman. An important role of the concierge physician is to guide his or her patients through the complexity of health care in a similar fashion.

A particular aspect of the Sewell service model that concierge medicine should seek to emulate is demonstrated by my own experience. I took my wife's car in for what I thought was a minor issue but the repair was going to take longer than I had anticipated. The service representative offered me a complimentary loan car, which I declined, thinking that it would be a simple enough matter to allow me to get home and then come back to pick up the car when it was ready. He then proposed to drive me home himself. It appeared that there were several people behind me waiting to be assisted, and I pointed this out to him. He replied, "Right now you are my most important customer."

> "Every system is perfectly designed to achieve the results that it gets."
>
> *(Berwick, 1996)*

Prioritization of the patient or customer is, similarly, a critical aspect of delivering high-quality medical care, but it requires a delivery structure—a system—that ensures the next patient or customer is not significantly inconvenienced. The smaller panel sizes—and concomitantly less hectic schedules—in concierge medicine help to allow adequate time for the needs and expectations of the immediate patient to be met with less likelihood of creating delays for the next patient. Taking the time to develop and implement the systems that enable such high levels of customer service is well worth it for any business—be it a car dealership or a medical practice. It is common wisdom that the cost of acquiring a new customer (or a new patient) is much greater than the cost of keeping an existing one. Most estimates are in the range of 5–25 times more for marketing and acquisition (Gallo, 2014). From another perspective, increasing customer retention rates by 5% increases profits by 25%–95% (Reichheld and Teal, 2001).

Uber

Uber is a slang word for "super," which is what the stock market thinks of this company (despite the recent turnover in senior management). Merriam-Webster adds to the definition: "to an extreme or excessive degree" (*Merriam-Webster*

Learner's Dictionary, 2017). Uber was founded in 2009 by Garrett Camp and Travis Kalanick, who took advantage of the business opportunity created by the advent of the smartphone and the general customer dissatisfaction with taxi services. Started with $200,000 in seed money, the company has been immensely successful and is now valued at up to $70 billion (Hartmans and McAlone, 2016; Sloan, 2017).

Essentially, Uber serves as a link between drivers, whom it classifies as independent operators (although this has been challenged by courts and commissions in some states and countries), and the public. This peer-to-peer relationship, called Uberization, is impacting other industries. Uber drivers and their company are disrupting the taxi industry by offering a more pleasant, personalized service. I cannot remember a cab driver opening and closing my door for me, yet Uber drivers do this routinely. They are uniformly polite and respectful. The fee may be a bit higher, but the payment is easy with a credit card on file.

Everything about the experience seems to surpass the experience of transportation in taxicabs. Most who try the Uber service stick with it (or with their competitor, Lyft), similar to those who try the concierge model. Concierge medicine has already established a foothold due to patient and provider dissatisfaction with aspects of traditional practice arrangements. Well-functioning concierge models are likely to continue to be disruptive to traditional medicine.

Disney

> "We don't put people in Disney, we put Disney in people."
>
> *(Lipp, 2013)*

The Disney Company has always been intensely focused on customer service. An "aggressively friendly" attitude is expected when employees interact with visitors. Walt Disney himself taught, "You can dream, create, design and build the best, the most wonderful place on earth, but it requires people to make that dream a reality" (JustDisney.com, 2017).

Disney culture extends from continually entertaining visitors to the ideal maintenance of its environment. If you have been to a Disney park, you must have noticed the impeccable cleanliness of the grounds. In Orlando, Florida, there are 70,000 employees who help to maintain that image. This includes not only the groundkeepers, but the actors, ride operators, and vendors. *Every* employee is expected to pick up trash and straighten chairs at *every* opportunity (Walt Disney World Resort, 2017).

Disney University was created to develop the world's most engaged, loyal, and consumer-centric employees in the world. The company hires for attitude, not aptitude, and it recruits, selects, and trains everyone the same way, regardless of the role they are hired to fill. Successful concierge physicians will have similar attributes—friendly, compassionate, and non-judgmental, in addition to the requisite competency and meticulousness.

Disney University also teaches excellence in service. They describe this as a true understanding of the customer's expectations and putting the right guidelines and service patterns in place to exceed them. They also refer to their customers as guests (Lipp, 2013). One of the hospitals in the Baylor Scott & White Health system also refers to its patients as guests. Concierge practices should consider, if not refer to, their clientele in similar fashion.

Effective communication is another important concept for Disney. Timeliness is stressed and extends to all rides, shows, and trains. If a train is late, even by a few seconds, the conductor is expected to explain to the guests on the train the reason for the delay. A "well-oiled" concierge practice should do the same. The front office staff will make the first impression. They must be friendly and communicate delays if they occur. It is important to remember that patients often feel vulnerable, sometimes even fearful and frightened. A friendly, caring face can shape and influence the health care experience in a positive way. Disney has figured this out with their guests.

Nordstrom

"Do whatever it takes to take care of the customer."

John W. Nordstrom *(Spector and McCarthy, 2012)*

Starting with a small shoe store in 1901, John W. Nordstrom built a company around a strong commitment to customer service. Blake W. Nordstrom, grandson of the founder, and chief executive officer since 2000, has since amplified this notion: "It's not about us being ranked on top or 'best in class.' It's about doing what's best for the customer. In fact, forget 'best in class,' the customer is constantly raising the bar, and since they are setting the standard, we're continually resetting ours upward" (Adams, 2013). This should be the attitude toward all patients but is especially important for those in the concierge world.

The Nordstrom Training Manual lists three key techniques (Spector and McCarthy, 2012):

1. View every customer interaction as a story opportunity.
2. Define service from the customer's point of view.
3. Exceed your customer's expectations.

The company likes to simplify this further and does so in their employee handbook:

We're glad to have you with our Company. Our number-one goal is to provide outstanding customer service. Set both your personal and professional goals high. We have great confidence in your ability to achieve them.

Nordstrom's Rules:
Rule # 1: Use your good judgment in all situations.
There will be no additional rules.

(Lutz, 2014)

Concierge practices must constantly strive for outstanding customer (patient) service. This is a recurrent agenda item in our Signature Medicine monthly staff meetings.

Ritz-Carlton

"We are Ladies and Gentlemen serving Ladies and Gentlemen."

Ritz-Carlton Motto *(Ritz-Carlton, 2017)*

This company aspires to provide the finest personal service and facilities. The ambience in its facilities is expected to be warm, relaxed, and refined. They teach their approaches and processes in a leadership center that is also available to other companies that desire to enrich their own cultures in the Ritz-Carlton tradition.

The Ritz-Carlton prescribes Three Steps of Service (Ritz-Carlton, 2017):

1. Address each customer with a warm and sincere greeting.
2. Use the guest's name. Anticipate and strive to fulfill each guest's needs.
3. Fond farewell. Give a warm good-bye and use the guest's name.

The Ritz-Carlton excels in exceeding the expectations of its customers. It keeps records on each customer's likes and dislikes. Going out of its way to please each guest is part of its culture. Its legendary service is anchored in four tenets:

1. Attention to Detail
   "The small things ARE the big things!"
2. Flawless Processes
   Consistency
3. An Emotional Connection
   Unique, Memorable, Personable
4. Random Acts of Kindness
   Develop WOW stories

All health care experiences are ideally "warm, relaxed, and refined," but concierge practices in particular should strive to exceed the expectations of their client base. The four tenets of the Ritz-Carlton have direct application to the concierge model.

Chapter 5

How to "Do" Concierge Medicine

The Patience Experience and Culture

What an individual experiences during an interaction with an organization depends heavily on the culture of the organization. Some organizations have a playful, upbeat culture. Southwest Airlines is famous for this. You may have heard a playful flight attendant announce, "In the event your oxygen mask drops down, first place the mask on yourself. Then pick your favorite child and fix theirs in place" (Mikkelson, 2005). Other organizations have a more serious, deliberate style. Detectives in police departments often emulate this approach, which is best exemplified by Sergeant Joe Friday of the television show *Dragnet*. He frequently pleaded, "Just the facts, ma'am."

Edgar Schein calls culture "a pattern of shared basic assumptions learned by a group as it solved its problems of external adaptation and internal integration" (Schein, 1985). In the specific context of health care, Forrester Research defines culture as a system of shared values and behaviors that focus employee activity on improving the patient experience—that is, "everything patients see, touch, feel, hear, and think about their interactions with the organization" (Johnson and Stern, 2017). In a culture that emphasizes quality and safety of care, employees will always assist patients when they get down from an examination table to prevent falls; take the time to explain the need for colonoscopies, mammograms, flu shots, pneumonia vaccines, and other preventive services that can improve health and save lives; and present a friendly, unrushed demeanor. Such actions build confidence in the provider and result in better understanding by the patient—both of which increase the likelihood that the patient will follow medical advice.

Because the service expectations are high in concierge practices, culture is important. This must be openly communicated among all employees, and examples of a strong culture must be cited. Signature Medicine has monthly meetings where satisfaction scores are reviewed and thoroughly discussed. Daily huddles at the start of each work day focus on the particular needs of each scheduled patient.

The Culture of the Clinic

"Leadership is practiced not so much in words as in attitude and in actions."

Harold S. Geneen *(Geneen and Moscow, 1985)*

Culture is strongly influenced by those at the top of an organization. If the lead physician or chief executive officer pays only lip service to the manner in which patients are treated, *Service Extraordinaire* will not occur. Culture is the atmosphere in which one works, and it extends to the way everyone is treated. If the environment is not collegial and friendly, the experience for the patient will not be either.

"Your mother was right: manners really are important. The environment the boss creates says a lot

about how he feels about himself and the people
who work for him."

Carl Sewell *(Sewell and Brown, 2002)*

My concierge medicine practice, Signature Medicine, rather
than operating independently, is part of a large, integrated
health care delivery system that has a strongly established culture of quality and safety. As a physician-in-training, I remember seeing then-chief executive officer (CEO) of the Baylor
Health Care System, Boone Powell, Jr., lean over and pick up
a discarded cup in one of the hospital hallways. Such example
setting from the top of a large organization trickles down, with
employees taking cues from their leaders.

The late W. W. ("Bill") Aston, a onetime utility company
executive and Baylor Health Care System trustee, taught
me valuable lessons through a medical instrument analogy
(Figure 5.1). He explained that a culture may be disciplined
or disordered depending upon the leader's example.
Employees take cues from their leaders and act accordingly.

"A good leader sets the temperature of the organization."

W. W. Aston

Figure 5.1   Setting the temperature of the organization. (From Terry
Morris - stock.adobe.com.)

This is not, of course, to say that the individual clinics and other entities within the larger health care system do not have their own subcultures, or that their individual leaders do not influence the values and behaviors within those entities just as much as system leadership does.

Signature Medicine has its own mission statement, crafted by our members and staff. It is prominently displayed both in our office and on our web page, where it stands as a reminder to our patients and to ourselves of our daily goal (Figure 5.2).

A critical aspect of the culture in a context such as a concierge medicine practice, where a relatively small number of people must work closely together on an ongoing basis, is demonstrating respect and appreciation for colleagues and all team members. Doing so in front of the patients can also help to build patient confidence in the abilities of the staff, which sets the tone for a pleasant patient experience and the fostering of additional relationships between the patient and the practice. This can in turn lead to greater information sharing

Figure 5.2 Signature Medicine mission. (From Dr. Winter's practice.)

and better quality care. For example, on a patient's first visit to the practice, I like to introduce my nurse in a way that recognizes her contributions to our teamwork-based approach to care. I might say, for example, "I want to introduce you to my nurse, who is the best caretaker I know. If you ever need anything, please do not hesitate to ask her." Over the years, I have found that it is not unusual for a patient to mention a concern to my staff that they may not mention to me. Maintaining multiple lines of communication enhances our opportunities to serve our customers.

Another way in which I like to foster a teamwork approach is by involving all our staff in the patient's care. Our front office employee makes a point to greet each patient by name and make light conversation while our records are updated to prepare for the visit. Our nurse then personally takes the patient into the examination room for an update on their history, medications, allergies, and current issues. She records this along with blood pressure, weight, and height before I enter the room. Of course, I could perform all of those activities myself, but involving staff builds trust in our practice's entire system, and connects and bonds my nurse and receptionist with the patient.

The success of our system was demonstrated to me by a patient at a social function. HB loudly told a gathered group, "I have access to the best health care in Dallas. I just call Dr. Winter's nurse. She is always available, knows the answer, or can quickly get back to me with advice from him." It was nice to hear that compliment which reinforces our teamwork approach toward health care.

Building staff rapport must, of course, extend beyond the interactions witnessed by patients. Opportunities to celebrate with the staff should not be missed. These can include employee birthdays, clinic anniversaries, service awards, and quality achievements. Monthly meetings for all also help to establish teamwork-based attitudes, especially when each team member has an agenda item to prepare and present. The result is not only a good work environment, but also better staff retention, which helps us to retain the collective organizational knowledge of our patients' histories, habits, and tendencies. This rapport building is not unique to the concierge medicine setting—although the less pressured schedule can certainly help accommodate it. Even in my previous clinic, I sometimes had staff leave and go elsewhere for a higher salary, only to return later because they preferred the friendly, collaborative atmosphere that we promoted and enjoyed.

"Huddles," in which the entire team reviews the day's schedule at the start of the day, are becoming commonplace in forward-thinking practices. For us, these are prompted by a printout of the daily schedule. We review who is coming in and what special services may be needed. Our practice adds to this by reviewing the previous day's work for follow up and any after hours calls that need to be addressed. In these sessions, we also often discuss employee family events to keep us all in touch. One member of our team has a grandson who is quite an athlete, and hearing about his accomplishments in his school team sports is always fun.

Another aspect of culture that can be tempting to trivialize, but is important for both the work environment and the patient experience we seek to cultivate, is the appearance of our facilities. Wilted flowers, an unclean environment, and out-of-date magazines give a negative impression of the office and the services that are rendered. Several of my patients through the years have commented how nice our facilities look. Some have even refused to go back to a specialist who failed to maintain a top-notch office. They ask, "If they let their office look shabby, how will their care of my health differ?"

Finally, one's culture can be refined and enhanced from the experiences of others. Press Ganey is a company that was founded more than 30 years ago to focus on patient experiences in health care (Press Ganey, 2017). Signature Medicine has been a member of this organization and earned

Figure 5.3   Signature Medicine Awards from Press Ganey.

its top patient experience award over multiple consecutive years. We are proud of this achievement but do not take it for granted. It is easy to become satisfied and complacent with one's work, and we guard against this carefully. At a recent group meeting, after Signature Medicine received its most recent award, we congratulated everyone on their efforts, but then immediately brainstormed what we could do in the next year to go even further to comfort and care for our patients (Figure 5.3).

The Art of Superlative Care?

"The day a company begins to be run for the benefit of the insiders, and not the benefit of the customers, is the day that the institution begins to die."

Peter Drucker *(Drucker Institute, 2013)*

> "Constantly improve. If you're not getter better, you're getting worse."
>
> **Anonymous**

Satisfied customers (read: patients) are one thing, but extraordinary care is another. Satisfied patients may stay with their doctor but a neighbor, friend, or relative can flip them to the care of another physician with a casual recommendation. On the other hand, patients who have experienced extraordinary care will return time after time. A buzz phrase currently making the rounds in health care is "Wowing the Patient." In other words, finding a way to surprise the patient with service above and beyond their expectations. This is not only good practice in general, but with the current consumerism movement (see discussion in Chapter 3, under "Physician Frustrations"), superlative access, communication, and follow through are becoming expectations, if not requisites.

There is an art to superlative care of patients. This includes impressing them with your attention, your thoroughness, and your compassion. Many physicians figure this out intuitively. Others learn this from parent organizations; for example, within HealthTexas Provider Network (HTPN), the Service Excellence Committee promulgates superlative care ideas and disseminates that to all member practices and providers. Satisfaction scores are monitored by this committee, and those with lower scores are coached or counseled or both. Our concierge physicians like to think that we have taken this to an even higher level. We frequently share stories and give tips to each other in attempt to do so.

The importance of service excellence and effective physician–patient communication in achieving good patient outcomes is often underestimated (Ha and Longnecker, 2010). Highly engaged patients are more likely to follow the advice and recommendations of their physicians. This includes obtaining recommended immunizations and disease screening procedures, such as mammograms and colonoscopies. Smoking cessation, control of blood pressure, and lowering of cholesterol levels are also more often achieved by highly satisfied patients (Alexander et al., 2012; Greene et al., 2015). In essence, service excellence results in healthier patients.

Smile Therapy?

☺ ☺ ☺ ☺ ☺

Skeptics denounce the focus of service excellence as "pandering to patients" that is not necessarily in the best interest of patients (Fischer, 2015; Nazario, 2012). Their accusation is that always striving to please patients can lead to excessive or inappropriate use of diagnostic tests, images, or procedures, as well as medications such as antibiotics and narcotics.

Certainly, pills are not always the answer. Too many adults today have the attitude that there is a pill for every malady—an attitude that can lead to too many pills for too few good reasons (Figure 5.4).

"Ask your doctor if taking a pill to solve all your problems is right for you."

Figure 5.4 A pill for every problem. (David Sipress/*The New Yorker* Collection/The Cartoon Bank.)

In the case of antibiotics, this creates risks that extend beyond the individual patient: overuse has led to resistance for many of the common bacterial organisms, and as a consequence we are seeing a resurgence of untreatable infections (Ventola, 2015). However, this argument is not often effective on sick patients who come to the physician's office convinced that only antibiotics will relieve the symptoms plaguing them (Hertz, 2014). More pertinent is information about how antibiotic treatment can upset the balance of necessary bacteria in our bodies. Excessive use can lead to life-threatening *Clostridium difficile* overpopulation and fungal and yeast infections. One of my patients, who—appropriately—required multiple courses of antibiotics, unfortunately developed severe Clostridia diarrheal illness that weakened his heart and almost resulted in his demise. I use him as an example to discourage other patients pleading for antibiotics that they do not need. Patiently explaining the risks of overuse is true service excellence in this context—not giving in to the patient's request, yet not brusquely refusing it in a manner that will make them likely to seek out another provider and try again.

Narcotics are another matter. They are a very effective way to alleviate severe, acute pain or a lingering cough. The downside, of course, is that they can become addictive. The current opiate crisis in our country demonstrates the importance of this understanding, and of monitoring patients' use of narcotics over time. An advantage to the concierge model is that it fosters the kind of long-term, close physician–patient relationship that enables an emerging addiction to be detected and addressed (Matthias et al., 2014). For example, DB is an elderly patient of mine with lots of back and joint issues who is also prone to bronchitis. Several years ago, my nurse and I noted that he was refilling his narcotic prescription with greater regularity. I called him to ask about his pain and cough. His response was startling: "My cough is gone and joints are doing pretty well right now. I find, though, that I get this lull in the afternoons and the prescription pill makes me feel better." He was surprised and appalled when I told him that he was addicted and experiencing symptoms of narcotic withdrawal.

Prescription sleeping pills also have downsides. They have their uses and work very well for folks after major operations, for example, or when they are traveling through several time zones. The problem is that regular use of sleep medications can lead to tolerance and the need for higher doses. With continued, frequent use, it is not uncommon for folks not to sleep well with them and not sleep at all without them.

The ABCs of Concierge Care

This chapter details some basics of performing extraordinary care. These lessons are particularly applicable to concierge models.

AIDET

The Studer Group, a health care consulting firm founded by Quint Studer, who was twice named in *Modern Healthcare*'s 100 Most Influential People in Healthcare list, created the AIDET® communication framework to help health care workers optimize service during an office visit (Studer Group, 2017; Rubin, 2014). The acronym AIDET stands for Acknowledge, Introduce, Duration, Explanation, and Thank You. The AIDET framework is often referred to as the "five fundamentals of communication" (Rubin, 2014) and represents a powerful way to communicate with patients, particularly when they are uncomfortable, nervous, or stressed in the physician's exam room.

Acknowledgment
Introductions
Duration

Explanation
Thank You

ACKNOWLEDGMENT helps to put the patient at ease. It starts with a warm smile and a pleasant greeting. "How are you doing?" can be confusing to patients. They may be in the office with a medical problem, so they are "not doing well." A more neutral greeting, such as "It is good to see you" or "It is nice to see you again" is more appropriate. Eye contact and using the patient's name or nickname enhance the interaction.

INTRODUCTIONS are important if the patient is new to the practice or if there are others in the room with whom you may not be familiar. The introduction can include name, professional background, skill set, and experience. For example, "My name is Dr. David Winter, I am an internal medicine specialist, I have been doing this for three decades, and I want to make sure that I meet your concerns and answer all of your questions today."

DURATION refers to setting expectations regarding the time set aside for the visit. Patients are often frustrated if the visit ends suddenly, before they can ask all of their questions. Any delay in seeing the physician should also be communicated. If call backs are anticipated to be needed to report test results, the timing of this should also be mentioned. Even though concierge practices are not usually rushed, there will be times when work-in appointments can stress the schedule. Duration can be an issue in those instances. My staff stays alert for these occasions and is quick to inform the patients. We are all careful to avoid the appearance that we have less time than they require.

EXPLANATION is a very important part of communication. Patients need to understand the diagnosis and treatment plan. It is important to remember that patients are often anxious and not always able to remember your instructions. Writing down every important instruction helps to ensure compliance. Also important is using words that our patients can understand, avoiding medical jargon. Helping patients to appreciate the reasoning behind a diagnosis and treatment plan is always important, and we liberally use examples, anatomical models, drawings, and diagrams. The simple phrase "Does this all make sense to you?" encourages further dialogue that might have been missed.

Concluding with those simple words, "THANK YOU," can reinforce a sense of respect and trust. This can be personalized: "I want to thank you for the opportunity to be a part of your health care team." This final principle is always appropriate. I often personalize this by saying something like, "I am so glad that you came today to give me the opportunity to help you with your issue."

After going through *acknowledge* and *introductions* fundamentals, a minute or two of casual conversation often helps to calm the patient. There is no need to rush to get to the chief concern. Once the conversation about the patient's issue begins, it is important that the physician maintains eye contact and remains relaxed and attentive. The average time to interruption by a physician is 18 seconds, according to a well-quoted study by Beckman and Frankel (1984). In the study, the patients reported that prior to interruption, they completed less than one-fourth of what they wanted to convey. Since 70%–80% of diagnoses are made by medical history alone, it behooves us to listen longer (Lown, 1999). Attentive listening also helps to build trust and confidence.

For long-standing concierge patients, the formalized principles of the AIDET acronym may be streamlined to allow for more informal conversation in which patients are encouraged to talk about something unrelated to their current visit. A comment about their family or hobbies allows them to relax and loosen up.

Access

Patients today seem less tolerant of waiting to see a doctor when they have a medical illness or a concern (Block,

2015). This is becoming increasingly important in all patient settings—and is particularly true in concierge medicine where patients have paid a retainer fee, at least partly to ensure that access to physician services is at their own convenience. At Signature Medicine, when patients call for appointments, we emphasize this by, instead of offering a time, asking, "When would YOU like to come in?"

I have also chosen to offer home visits as part of my concierge practice. This service not only meets the patients' expectations of the convenience they paid for, but allows me to gain further insight into the patient and enjoy the relaxed environment, thereby improving the care I provide them. It is just as easy for me to stop by a patient's office, when requested.

In my particular case, providing patients with the convenient access necessary for concierge care sometimes has to be worked around my two jobs and two offices—only one of which was designed for clinical encounters. Recently, I had a patient request a visit in the afternoon, when I am typically in my administrative office. He was directed there and, after a brief greeting, started talking about a pain in his groin. This sounded like an inguinal hernia and required an examination for diagnosis. There is a problem with this in my administrative office: a see-through glass door. To escape onlookers and mutual embarrassment, we found an empty conference room with wooden doors and privacy (Figure 5.5).

Figure 5.5 Patient privacy is important. (From Antonioguillem - stock. adobe.com.)

The exam confirmed my suspicions, and I sent him off to the surgeon for repair. Such situations require flexibility on both my part and my patients'—and that flexibility is crucial for the convenient access that is such an important part of concierge medicine.

Hospital rounds are also included in our model. I routinely admit my own patients. They are certainly comfortable with a familiar face, and coordinating the care of complicated cases with multiple specialists is important for optimal outcomes. Years ago, most internal medicine physicians admitted and cared for all of their patients. Paralleling the move to specialization, today the vast majority of primary care physicians refer their patients to hospital specialists (hospitalists) when admission to the hospital is required. The challenge is coordinating their care before and after the hospital stay. And then there are those very important decisions, such as when to call off aggressive treatment and pivort to comfort care. Such discussions are easier with a familiar physician who knows the patient and family's wishes.

Computer Challenges

As is commonly discussed in health care circles, computers can add a challenge to good communication. A computer keyboard and monitor positioned between the physician and the patient can serve as a barrier, stifling productive discourse. So how does one maintain eye contact when an electronic medical record requires attention? Several obvious answers come to mind: complete computer entries after leaving the patient's room (not very efficient), dictate into voice recognition software, or use a scribe. With practice, most physicians can more efficiently dictate than type into the medical record. Dictating in front of a patient can be done smoothly if the patient is invited to listen in. I like to then ask them if I have appropriately captured their thoughts.

Another technique uses additional personnel called scribes who quietly accompany the physician in the examination room and record pertinent data in the computer while the physician focuses on the patient. Entrepreneurial companies are now offering long-distance scribes who listen in with "Alexa™-type" devices or observe the encounter with Google Glasses. Successful use of voice recognition software or the services of scribes benefits both concierge and traditional models of health care delivery.

What about typing on the computer while talking to the patient? This can be done, but it is important to stay facing the patient and to look up from the computer screen frequently. If there is a need to record an important and lengthy piece of information, this should be acknowledged. I often say something like: "That sounds important, so let me take time to put that into your record."

Modern portable software allows me to deliver medical advice in any location. Our computer system has separate apps for my smartphone and tablet. With either of these, I can securely look up a summary of a patient's chart, call in prescriptions, and even document the encounter by dictating into my phone and sending that directly, and securely, into the patient's electronic health record.

Listening Longer

In the harried context of a traditional fee-for-service practice, many physicians, toward the conclusion of a patient visit, will be tempted to avoid asking, "Do you have any other questions?" The fear is of prolonging the visit unnecessarily—although, in my experience, that hardly ever happens. In fact, most patients respond by saying, "No, I think we covered it all." On the infrequent occasion when this question has prompted the patient to raise an additional issue, it has often turned out to be something that I either needed to hear to clinch the diagnosis, or would have required additional discussion via telephone or e-mail.

In concierge medicine, there is usually ample time to discuss all issues that patients bring to the appointment. Even though time constraints are less of a problem in concierge models, prompting patients can still be worthwhile. After a series of questions about a patient's history, medications, and allergies, and a review of the function of each organ system, I routinely ask, "What are you most concerned about in regard to your health?" This often leads to an issue that did not come up in the routine review.

Extended Visits, Last-Minute Visits, and Talkative Patients

Some patients just take longer and seem to do so most every time. The advantage to the relationships that concierge medicine fosters, together with the more flexible schedule, is that my staff and I come to know who these patients are and simply block out the additional time that experience tells us will be needed for them. For example, I have one patient who comes in every four months for a thorough discussion of his nine major chronic illnesses. We allow two hours for the visit as it usually takes an hour and a half to go over all the topics. We can then spend additonal time talking about our mutual hobby, fishing. In a traditional fee-for-service practice, where blocking out that additional time means foregone revenue from the appointments that could otherwise have been scheduled, these verbose patients tend to be labeled "difficult." The difficulty is the havoc they can wreak on a day structured to maximize use of standard 15-minute appointments. That problem does not (or certainly should not) exist in concierge models.

Such adaptation can be challenging for last-minute appointments, even in the context of the less hectic concierge medicine schedule. As mentioned, when patients ask for an appointment, we try to always answer in the affirmative. Occasionally, my staff receives a call asking for an appointment for a minor issue on an unusually busy day. Rather than decline an appointment time, they offer to let me speak with them. Often, I can meet their needs with advice over the phone. When this is not possible, we try to schedule any last-minute appointments as the final appointment of the morning or afternoon, which generally enables me to stay on schedule for other patients.

When patients are due for an extended visit (at Signature Medicine, we attempt to have such a visit at least annually), but want to come in urgently because of a new concern, we tell them to come right in for their new problem. Unless we have ample time then to go over all of their issues, new and old, we take care of the urgent need and use the opportunity to schedule the extended visit for another day so as not to interfere with other scheduled patients.

Forgetful, Stressed Patients

It is safe to assume that patients are likely to be anxious when in a doctor's office. As a consequence, they commonly have difficulty concentrating on advice and instructions. We try to set the tone so that this does not happen. Nonetheless, it is a good idea for physicians to write down anything of importance and hand this to them for reinforcement. This can also be done with computer printed instructions, but I try to write down something on paper for almost every patient visit. Patients, I have found, like walking out with written instructions, and this definitely curtails phone calls to clarify what they are supposed to do. Dr. Leslie Moore, a pediatrician, introduced me to that concept when our children were very young. At each well-baby visit, he would handwrite a note to summarize the visit. As I rarely found time to attend the appointments, I learned to look forward to his written comments.

Patients have been known to show up on the wrong day, and are understandably embarrassed. They may be convinced that they have the correct appointment, but rather than add to their mortification, or needlessly debate the appointment date, we take the high road. Blame is not important. We take the stance that the mistake is ours (it usually is not), apologize, and make time to see the patient while they are there. We do this even if they realize and admit that they are there on the wrong day. This is diffi-cult to do in a busy, traditional office practice when every appointment slot is filled. The concierge schedule allows more flexibility. We offer coffee, water, or a soft drink if we have other scheduled patients and the patient who arrived on the wrong day cannot be seen immediately.

Irritable Patients

It should not be surprising to find patients grumpy or irritable when they are ill and do not feel well. It may be tempting to breeze through these patients to get to more pleasant ones, but that would be a mistake. It is important to ignore the ten-dency to speed through the visit. This is a good opportunity to demonstrate compassion and empathy. Identifying with negative vibes often helps. For example, one could say, "I can see that you are not happy with your condition, let me see if I can help."

The Importance of Teamwork

Many elderly and even some younger patients today have a bevy of physicians whose offices they frequent. Physicians who specialize in organs (cardiologists, gastroenterologists, nephrologists, dermatologists), symptoms (pain management, psychiatry), and procedures (surgeons) all bring special tal-ents to patients. Finding ways to coordinate and focus on the entire patient's needs can be challenging in modern medicine. A pertinent analogy is the teamwork required in the game football (Figure 5.6).

Figure 5.6 Health care teamwork. (From Aspen Photo/Shutterstock.com.)

A primary care physician should serve as the medical quarterback in health care (Society of General Internal Medicine, 2017). It takes extra time to coordinate with specialists, reconcile medications, and review hospital and emergency department visits. Complicated patients can overwhelm a busy primary care physician in a traditional practice. The concierge model allows for more time to synchronize the care of the patient (Figure 5.7).

Health and Telemedicine

Real-time video conferencing is now available as an alternative to office visits. A picture transmitted electronically can be pivotal for a medical diagnosis. One of the barriers for these types of interaction is reimbursement, which varies between states and payers (Yang, 2016). Concierge medicine with its retainer fee obviates the need for this reimbursement. When patients call and attempt to describe a skin condition, I have them send me a picture. One recent patient was concerned

Figure 5.7 Primary care physician as quarterback. (From Richard Paul Kane/Shutterstock.com.)

about bed bugs that appeared after a recent hotel stay. The patient transmitted a picture which confirmed his diagnosis and led to the following advice: "Take diphenhydramine (Benadryl) capsules, apply hydrocortisone cream, and avoid that hotel room in the future."

Online dermatology services perform a similar function. One of my patients came into the office with a concern about a rash. After examination, I explained that he had eczema and that it would respond to a cortisone cream. He then admitted that he had gone to a web-based dermatology site the night before and obtained the same information and advice. "Just checking out the accuracy of the service," he said. (The dermatology website's, or mine?)

Scheduling Tricks

Mastering appointment schedules is an art. It can be managed for the benefit of the physician or for the benefit of the patients. Some offices, encouraged by the physician, rigidly control the schedule to avoid work-in patients who might generate a hectic environment. Sometimes it is the staff members themselves who want to make sure that they do not miss their lunch break or work past five o'clock. Concierge models must focus on what is best for the patient and not for the staff. This may mean coming in early, staying late, or visiting the patient at home.

Concierge practices are not immune to busy days—though they occur much less often than at traditional practices—and it is important to have appointment slots available for urgent visits. We always try to keep time available for those last-minute requests. In the event that a day's schedule is full, coming early or working through lunch is always an option. Often, an office visit can be avoided, as I described earlier, by talking to the patient on the phone and addressing the concerns. With the concierge model, there is no need or financial incentive to have patients come to the office unnecessarily.

Empathy

> "Empathetic care resonates with the noblest values of all clinicians."
>
> **Thomas H. Lee, MD** *(Lee, 2016)*

It is an indictment of health care and a plague on our industry when other businesses seem to exceed the empathy experienced in the health care industry. The Disney Company is passionate about timeliness, cleanliness, and excellence in service for their "guests." Nordstrom teaches its employees to "do whatever it takes to take care of the customer." The Ritz-Carlton stresses attention to detail, flawless processes, an emotional connection, and random acts of kindness. Health care in recent decades has stressed the application of science, but has empathy been neglected? Certainly many physicians and other health care workers demonstrate empathy frequently, but why not all the time?

Thomas H. Lee challenges those of us in health care: "We are living in a Golden Age of Medicine, but it doesn't feel that way." He writes about this in his book *An Epidemic of Empathy in Healthcare*, emphasizing an imperative to deliver compassionate care at every opportunity. "Organizations that help their personnel do that will be rewarded both with business success and with the pride that can result from an epidemic of empathy" (Lee, 2016).

When patients are ill or injured, they often feel vulnerable, and sometimes scared. Soothing their anxieties should be paramount in the care that we deliver. Sir Luke Fildes' 1887 painting *The Doctor* epitomizes the thoughtful care and concern that patients deserve (Figure 5.8).

Figure 5.8 "The Doctor" by Sir Luke Fildes. (From http://www.thefamousartists. com/luke-fildes/the-doctor. ©Tate, London 2017.)

The burdens of modern medicine for providers were chronicled in Chapter 1. "Hamster wheel" work schedules often leave little time for unhurried, deliberate discussions with patients. Physicians may harbor great respect and concern for patients' feelings, but in a rushed practice, the patient may see little evidence of this. The pace of concierge medicine offers more opportunities for conversation, but there is more to conveying concern and understanding than just patiently listening. It takes active listening, a calm and relaxed demeanor, and the demonstration of compassion.

You might ask about the time required to answer every thought and concern a patient brings to a doctor visit. Even in a busy practice, not every patient at every visit requires lengthy and exhaustive explanations. Usually, only a few patients need extra attention on any given day. This is an important understanding as there are not enough waking hours to talk at length with every patient, even in a concierge practice. Concentrating on those who need more time is important. New diagnoses, emotional issues, and unexpected outcomes often require unhurried, focused attention. These opportunities to build a relationship of trust and respect must be heeded. Patients need to know that you will be there for them when they need you.

It also benefits caregivers to become patients. I was rewarded this experience when I tore my rotator cuff on the ski slopes of Colorado several years ago. A terrific surgeon guided me through the process from diagnosis, to the operating room, through physical therapy. I strived to pay close attention during my follow-up office visits as he explained what I needed to do to maximize my results. Nonetheless, on several occasions, after he left the room, I had to ask his nurse to repeat his instructions and came to appreciate the difficulty concentrating when in front of a physician in an exam room.

I also distinctly remember his words prior to surgery: "I can fix your shoulder in 18 minutes." Worried about returning to work, the recovery, and whether I would ever ski again, I found great comfort in his words, only to become disillusioned later when I realized that it would take 12 months of daily exercises and therapy to totally regain the function of my shoulder.

Going through the entire process, I appreciated the nurses and aides who seemed to always calm and comfort me. I also remember those who were abrupt and curt. For all of us in health care, an important goal should be always to consider the feelings of our patients.

> "People don't care how much you know until they know how much you care."
>
> **Theodore Roosevelt**

Patients are aware that modern medicine is capable of many great things—conquering illnesses that were previously untreatable, for example—but they often worry that their feelings may be left in the lurch. I recently saw an anxious young man who had been to an ear, nose, and throat specialist; a neurologist; and a vascular specialist. He was having dizzy spells and was convinced he was going to become disabled. He confided that his mother remains paralyzed on one side from the results of a stroke. On examination, he displayed a classic fluttering of eyes called nystagmus when I laid his head back and to the left. This was accompanied by marked dizziness, and he became frightened. As I performed the Epley maneuver, his symptoms abated. "What did you do?" he asked, incredulously. I brought out an anatomic model of the ear and spent time explaining how a crystal in the semi-circular canal of the ear can produce his symptoms and how we were able to move the crystal out of the area to make the symptoms go away. He listened attentively and then calmly said, "Thank you. Now I understand." I suspect that others had tried to explain what was going on with him, but he needed a more thorough, unhurried explanation.

I have never felt that a patient wasted my time. In fact, many are unnecessarily concerned that they are consuming too much of my time and that they may be keeping me from someone else who may need my services. Just like that service representative at Carl Sewell's car dealership (Chapter 4), I want my patients to understand and feel that when they are in front of me, they are my most important patient.

If compassion relates to concern for the suffering or misfortune of others, and empathy is the ability to understand and share the feelings of others, then we need to have both in health care. We must have compassion for all those who suffer and empathy for those to whom we attend. Empathy is an important element of caring and is often long remembered. I am continually surprised when patients start a conversation with me by saying, "Doctor, I will never forget what you told me years ago." Similarly, medical students whom I have tutored and nurses with whom I have worked are always observing and patterning. Our measured example can help to fulfill Dr. Lee's pursuit for an "epidemic of empathy in health care" (Lee, 2016). Concierge models are ideally suited to lead the way. This requires us to always be patient, humble, compassionate, and empathetic (Lee and Cosgrove, 2014).

Prevention in Concierge Models

Many years ago, a strong emphasis in the practice of medicine was on caring. There were not many cures; treatments were primarily for comfort. As more effective diagnostic measures and therapies became available, treatment became more of a focus (Greenhalgh et al., 2015). A newer strategy involves preventing injury and illness in the first place (Lushniak et al., 2015). Prevention has been shown often to be more effective and more efficient than the treatment of more established medical problems (Egan et al., 2010; Goldman and Cook, 1984; Lavizzo-Mourey, 2012; Moser 1983). Concierge practices place great emphasis on prevention.

Prevention in health care means taking steps to avoid illness and injuries. Flu shots, pneumonia vaccines, and tetanus shots can prevent infections. Removing trip hazards in the home can prevent injuries from falls. Countless studies have demonstrated that those who eat correctly and have regular exercise habits can avoid medical conditions such as diabetes and hypertension. I have personally witnessed patients who met the diagnostic criteria for early onset diabetes or hypertension, yet have had those diagnoses resolve after a period of dieting, exercising, and losing weight.

Here is the list of important items that physicians stress to keep patients healthy:

PREVENTIVE MEASURES FOR GOOD HEALTH
- Keep up to date on recommended immunizations.
- Maintain a healthy diet.
- Exercise regularly.
- Strive for the appropriate weight for your frame.
- Avoid tobacco.
- Drink alcohol in moderation.
- Take prescription medications as recommended.
- Risky behavior? Don't take the risk.

How can a physician get patients to follow all these measures? There are advantages to concierge models. Without time constraints, longer in-office conversations are not a problem. It is also easy for my nurse or me to drop by a patient's house to administer a vaccine or draw blood to recheck cholesterol or glucose levels. As mentioned in Chapter 1, house calls provide an added benefit for patients: important insights into their lifestyles can be gained by the physician.

Osteoporosis afflicts an estimated 16% of women and 4% of men over 50 years of age (National Center for Health Statistics, 2017). Calcium and vitamin D may forestall the condition, but exercise is also important. Bones get stronger when subjected to regular exercise. Stronger bones are less likely to become thin and break. Periodic bone density tests allow us to assess our patients' status regarding skeleton framework.

There are other reasons that exercise is particularly important as we age. When a patient who is 70 years of age or
older requires hospitalization—for any reason: appendectomy,
knee replacement, or car collision injuries—it is common for
them to recover more slowly than younger folks. Enforced bed
rest adds to recovery challenges. It is not uncommon for the
elderly to recover from a brief hospital stay but remain too
weak to return home. Several weeks or more in a skilled nursing facility or rehabilitation hospital are often required. In contrast, elderly patients who exercise regularly are more likely to
return right back home.

RB had the habit of walking for an hour every day. He
enjoyed doing this with his wife, and it was a part of their
daily ritual. I liked to emphasize that this was good for his
health and that of his wife. At age 82, he came down with
a nasty case of pneumonia that required hospital admission
and an operation to remove a diseased segment of lung. Many
were surprised when he went home five days after his operation to resume his walking routine. A less fit octogenarian
would have needed several weeks in a rehabilitation facility to
regain strength and endurance. His fitness from regular exercise prevented a prolonged recovery.

Exercise habits are often formed early in life. High school
and college kids should be encouraged to develop them as
part of their weekly routine. Newly retired patients can also
often be converted to a regular exercise regimen with a few
focused discussions. These should be spotlighted during visits
to physicians, as is commonly done in concierge practices.

Exercise also plays a role in the prevention of heart attacks,
strokes, and even some forms of cancer. As many as 250,000
deaths per year in the United States are attributable to a lack
of regular physical activity (Buttar et al., 2005; Myers, 2003;
Sculco et al., 2001).

JH is a fit, productive mother and wife who is afflicted with
severe, recurrent major depression. She has required several
hospitalizations for this. Between bouts of depression, you

would not recognize any signs of a mental health issue in this vibrant, outgoing lady. An important component of her well-being is exercise. We witnessed the importance of this after a sports injury. A hamstring tear limited her ability to exercise several years ago, resulting in a flare-up of depression necessitating intensive treatment in a psychiatric hospital. She and I are now even more aware of the importance that her regular exercise habits play in preventing recurrences.

Prevention is important in regard to diabetes. The epidemic of obesity in our country is shadowed by an epidemic of diabetes (Albrecht et al., 2017; Menke et al., 2015). Our parents' admonition to eat everything on our plates has not worked well for many. I try to point out healthy choices and portion control when patients are ready to listen. We also have a dietician available for more detailed discussions. Many people believe that they are on healthy diets, yet find that they have room for significant improvement. We have patients record everything they eat over a typical three-day period. They are asked to write down the food and drink items and the approximate amounts. It is often surprising to see what our dietician discovers from such a food diary. Improper eating habits are the source of diabetes and many other illnesses (Chipkin et al., 2001; Colberg et al., 2010; Gaskins et al., 2007).

Prevention also includes screening services such as mammograms, Pap smears, and colonoscopies. There is typically more time to discuss the importance of these in a concierge practice. Our staff also runs lists of patients who are due for such services and sends out notifications between our patients' office visits.

Is your blood pressure or sugar level within an optimal range or is an adjustment necessary? Have you had a tetanus shot in the last 10 years? Is your colonoscopy or mammogram due? Keeping track of these things is important, and having a system that notifies the patient to schedule needed services is key. Such systems are easier to manage in a concierge practice.

Management of Chronic Illnesses

Proper management of chronic conditions benefits from focused attention, frequent communication, and accessibility. Concierge models should easily allow for these. The skill set of the physician also plays a role here. It may be difficult to ascertain, but a good concierge physician has advanced skills in diagnosis and treatment. These skills are enhanced as physicians work in the practice of medicine. You would not expect a fresh-out-of-school car mechanic to have all the answers for your broken-down car. Similarly, a physician with experience may offer advantages.

Chapter 6

Barriers to the Transition to Concierge Medicine

It is not easy for physicians to transition from a traditional medical practice into concierge medicine. Some physicians are tempted to start a concierge practice but are not sure that their patient base will support this. Others worry about the requirement of having to be more available to their patients. I have heard several comments along these lines:

"I can't be on call all the time!"
"I need to spend time with my family."
"I value my time off and do not want to be disturbed."
"What about my wine collection?"
"Can I be in concierge medicine and still drink wine?"
    (As we tell our patients, "Everything in moderation.")

There are also those who decry the whole idea of a concierge practice. Two-tiered medicine and elitism are mentioned. And certainly, the current shortage of primary care physicians will be exacerbated if there is a mass exodus from busy mature practices into the smaller panels of concierge practices. More primary care practices are sorely needed in this country, and the current training programs have yet to gear up to meet this demand.

When physicians exit an established group, they leave behind a number of patients who do not follow. It is not unusual for a busy physician to downsize from 2,000–3,000 patients to 200–300 patients during the transition to concierge medicine. Ideally, arrangements are made for patients who do not choose the new concierge practice to relocate to another physician's practice. HealthTexas Provider Network (HTPN) performs an assessment of capacity in the geographic proximity, and delays or discourages the opening of new concierge practices until this capacity is found to be adequate. Our goal is to prevent any patients from being stranded or left wanting.

Existing patients of a physician who leaves a traditional practice for the concierge model are often anxious about leaving their physician. They may push for early appointments with their newly adopted physician, which can strain the schedules of those physicians. The accepting physicians themselves may have mixed feelings about taking over the care of patients from another physician who has adopted a different practice style. Ideally, there is coordination when a physician transitions to a reduced panel of patients.

Chapter 7

Concierge Lessons for Non-Concierge Physicians

The concierge model has produced ideas that have migrated into traditional medical practices. Concierge practices serve as a learning laboratory where clinic operations such as patient flows and enhanced communication are refined. In the HealthTexas Provider Network (HTPN), when concierge models develop, other practices often adopt many of the techniques. For example, e-mail access to a physician is standard in concierge practices and is now more common in all practices. Office schedules in traditional office practices that minimize wait times are being emphasized. Attention to preventive services and immunizations, between office visits, is becoming more common. The teamwork philosophy using multiple members of the team has been refined in progressive concierge practices and then spread to our other practices.

An example of an important technique, improved upon in concierge practices, involves efficient use of the time that a patient spends in the office. From the moment the patient walks into our office, attention is focused on minimizing idle time. If I am running behind, the staff puts the patient's time to good use by reviewing medications, allergies, and new issues. Coffee or water are offered, and any needed immunizations are administered. The concierge movement itself does not get full credit for all of these enhancements, but its presence certainly has wielded an influence. There are indeed innovative initiatives in traditional practices that have evolved, but change is difficult for established models. As one of my previous partners voiced, "I don't have time to learn how to be more efficient."

The luxury of extra time with patients can have long-term benefits for patients and providers. One challenge in traditional practices is that it is easier to fulfill patient requests than to explain why their requests are not justified. It takes less time to write a prescription for an unwarranted antibiotic or to order an unneeded magnetic resonance imaging (MRI) scan than to spend the time to explain why these may not be in their best interests.

My brother, Larry, made this clear to me some time ago. He had gone to see his physician asking for antibiotics to treat the symptoms of a cold. After an examination, the physician announced to my brother that he did not need antibiotics. Though he was a bit abrupt, the doctor did mention that antibiotics were not necessary in his case, and he explained how they might even cause harm. Larry left disappointed but later reflected on the doctor's words and came to the conclusion that his doctor did him a favor. He has since not wasted time visiting doctors for cold viruses.

Patients may think they know exactly what they need and become argumentative when their requests are not honored. A useful approach is to give them what they want while explaining the actual circumstances for which an antibiotic, for example, might be helpful. Here is how this might work: as I write out the prescription, I explain that if I were them, I would not take the antibiotic unless I developed one or more specific symptoms. I write these down on a separate piece of paper. I then hand them the prescription along with the note of instructions. This approach has been demonstrated to reduce the likelihood that the patient will fill the unnecessary prescription while also satisfying the patient's request (Fleming-Dutra et al., 2016).

Additional time spent with patients produces other benefits. It can allow opportunities to gather important information. As I was wrapping up an appointment with one of my patients, he announced, "Come to think of it, I have been wondering whether to mention some discomfort that I have noticed when walking up stairs." Sure enough, he was experiencing chest pain from a partially blocked coronary artery. His condition was caught early enough that we are able to treat him with medication; he did not require surgery or stents. Relaxed, unrushed appointments can make a difference!

As physicians and patients get to know each other over a number of years, their relationship naturally builds. Trust and confidence are key factors in the success of a physician–patient relationship, and these take time to develop. They can develop more rapidly with extended visits in a concierge setting. Physicians in traditional practices might be alert for opportunities to enhance relationships. I am convinced that this can lead to better outcomes for patients.

Chapter 8

Concierge Medicine in a Health Care System

Does concierge medicine belong in a health care system? If the system supports a full range of health care delivery services, then yes. If such systems support a variety of different medical practices, the answer is yes. When wellness programs are a part of a health care system, yes. In a large population of patients with diverse needs, yes again.

A concierge medicine program takes care of patients in a special way. Its steady growth in America portends its endurance in the national health care system, but this does not mean it will become the predominant model of primary care. As the recently retired chief executive officer of Baylor Scott & White Health (BSWH), Joel Allison, is fond of saying, "Concierge medicine fits within a menu of services that we offer to our patients."

Similar to the many independent urgent care centers and free-standing emergency departments, concierge medicine programs have typically developed outside health care systems. The problem with this for hospitals is downstream referrals. Without some type of affiliation or loyalty, patients who visit non-aligned clinics (or non-aligned concierge practices) can be directed away from their preferred hospitals. For example, if a patient's hospital of choice is brand A, but they visit a local urgent care center for abdominal pain, they may end up at hospital B if that pain turns out to be due to appendicitis. This, of course, is not good for hospital A, but can also have substantial financial consequences for the patient. If a patient's preference for hospital A is based on it being "in network" for their health plan, while hospital B is not, the cost difference to the patient is likely to be significant. If the patient's trusted physician is not on staff at hospital B, the patient will also lose guidance and insight into the specialists that might be important.

To counter inadvertent loss of their patient base, organized health care systems have developed multiple avenues for patient care:

ACCESS POINTS FOR HEALTH CARE SYSTEMS
1. Primary care clinics
2. Specialty care clinics
3. Physical therapy clinics
4. Urgent care clinics
5. Emergency departments
6. Imaging centers
7. Laboratory services
8. Fitness centers
9. Dietary services
10. Concierge care practices

These varied access points exist to help keep patients within the system. Concierge practices sponsored by health care systems are expected to refer to hospitals, imaging centers, laboratory services, and other physicians associated with the network.

The advantages of concierge practices in health care systems also accrue to the systems in other ways. Concierge patients rely upon their physicians for advice when specialty referrals are needed. It therefore behooves health care systems to inventory concierge practices and encourage their allegiance. Tighter alignment results when the health care system sponsors or employs concierge physicians.

The affiliation of concierge medicine practices with hospital and health care systems can be modeled after affiliations between hospitals and health care systems and traditional physician practices. The relationship between BSWH and Signature Medicine exemplifies how this can be done. BSWH hospitals and Signature Medicine physician practices have collaborated on initiatives that promote quality, accessibility, affordability, chronic disease management, preventive health, and coordinated care across a continuum. A list of specific clinical quality improvement initiatives arising from this alignment follows:

CLINICAL QUALITY IMPROVEMENT INITIATIVES

- Smoking cessation
- Cholesterol reduction
- Immunization compliance
- Hypertension control
- Acute myocardial infarction management
- Chronic obstructive lung disease management
- Pneumonia treatment

All have been studied and defined through specific processes of care. Integration has been shown to lead to better care in the ambulatory, inpatient, and post-acute care environments; faster uptake of technology and specifically health information technology; and a stronger shared ability to improve population health (Baird et al., 2014; Hwang et al., 2013). The relationship between BSWH and Signature Medicine—along with other HealthTexas Provider Network (HTPN) practices—also enabled them to share experiences with and resources for performance measurement and reporting, including pay-for-performance programs that tie portions of hospital leaders' and physicians' reimbursement to this performance (HealthTexas Provider Network, 2016; Terry 2011; Winter 2001).

In addition to affiliation with hospitals or integrated delivery systems, concierge medicine practices may participate in accountable care organizations (ACOs). The concept behind ACOs resides within the word "accountable," meaning that the participating providers are responsible for all outcomes, including total cost of care. The federal government defines ACOs as "groups of doctors, hospitals, and other health care providers, who come together voluntarily to give coordinated high quality care to their patients" (Centers for Medicare and Medicaid Services, 2017a). Keeping patients within the system avoids the profligacy that unfortunately exists in today's health care. The medical profession has a long-standing tradition of self-regulation, and responds better to internally developed incentives (such as timely feedback of performance data on clinically meaningful measures) than to external motivators (such as financial rewards or penalties tied to overly complex dashboards of measures that do not intuitively connect to better patient outcomes) (Madara and Burkhart, 2015). The collective BSWH system has, for example, developed internal protocols for the treatment of sinus and ear infections that appropriately limit unnecessary use of antibiotics, and the system provides regular performance feedback to physicians on their compliance with these protocols.

Back pain protocols are another example of how standards developed and enforced across a diverse network of affiliated providers can improve care. Left to individual specialties, back pain is treated in diverse ways. Pain management doctors may more frequently recommend injections, physical medicine specialists may prefer physical therapy, and surgeons are trained to operate. How a patient is treated may therefore very much depend on whom they first contact. Most back complaints are, at least initially, seen by family practice and internal medicine physicians, be it in traditional practice settings or concierge practices. In an affiliated network or ACO that includes providers spanning all these specialties, a standardized clinical pathway or protocol can be developed to help guide back pain patients into the most appropriate treatments for their needs regardless of the point at which they initially access the system, optimizing care and eliminating unnecessary costs.

Concierge practices can also be fertile grounds for philanthropic donations. It is not unusual for grateful patients to make donations or bequests to hospital systems in honor of their physicians. They may go beyond this and set up their own foundations. Several years ago, one of my faithful patients asked me to meet him at a restaurant for lunch. He was always a lively conversationalist, so I readily agreed and adjusted my schedule accordingly. Not knowing his motive, I was surprised when he announced that he was setting up a medical research foundation and wanted me to be in charge of it. I was intrigued but initially resisted the added responsibility. It has since become a labor of love, and I quite enjoy directing grants to deserving research projects.

Identification with a trusted hospital brand benefits concierge physicians by adding to the credibility of the practice. Furthermore, the intricacies of setting up the concierge model can be handled by hospital administrative staff, allowing the physician to concentrate on patient care. It also can foster referrals to the concierge practices themselves: Hospital administrators and executives are frequently asked for recommendations regarding health care issues, and they can identify and recommend patients who would favor and potentially benefit from a concierge practice.

Where the affiliation is with a not-for-profit hospital system (e.g., BSWH) with a ministry-focused mission, the concierge practice may be encouraged or required to implement programs like the "scholarship" program described in Chapter 1, to enable access for patients who cannot afford the retainer fee. Such programs both help to counter the perception of concierge medicine as elitist, and expand the potential for lessons to be learned from concierge models that can be generalized to traditional and community clinics serving diverse patient populations (Gunderman, 2016). These programs also provide models or gateways for the introductions of a wider range of practice models that include smaller, sliding fee structures that make concierge-type approaches more affordable to lower- and middle-income patients. As argued previously, such concierge models can be expected to improve access and compliance with recommended preventive health care and chronic disease management (Portman and Romanow, 2008).

Studies of patient outcomes in concierge practices have reported lower emergency department utilization and reduced hospital readmission rates for serious illnesses—which reduces the overall costs of care (Klemes et al., 2012; Musich et al., 2014; Musich et al., 2016). If these reports are validated by studies in a broader population of patients, health care delivery organizations may seek to provide personalized, preventive medicine (what some call "concierge for all" or "concierge for the masses") (Feinberg et al., 2015) for much larger populations.

The Future of Health Care

Health care in the next decade will be different. Technology, economics, regulations, and demographics all are dictating changes. Whatever you think about health care in America, our costs seem needlessly high compared to those of other countries—especially since we are not producing longer life expectancies or better quality of life overall (The Commonwealth Fund, 2017). Many estimate that as much as 30% of health care expenditure represents waste that could be eliminated (Berwick and Hackbarth, 2012). Annual health care costs in the United States for a family of four are estimated to be over $25,000 (Munro, 2016). Even though a portion of that health care cost is often paid for by employers, it is still more than many can afford.

The political environment in America in 2017 is pushing for changes. What those changes will be is uncertain, but disruption and disarray are expected. Health care systems and physicians are likely to be pulled in different directions. Change is always challenging. Physicians themselves can be particularly resistant to change, partially as a result of their extensive and rigorous training that stresses consistency regarding the regimens that they have learned.

Additionally, the American population is aging, placing additional stressors on the health care system. Baby boomers are reaching age 65 at a rate of more than 10,000 per day (Fact Tank, 2010). Aging Americans often require more office visits, procedures, and medications. Traditional medical practices with their abbreviated office visits are not well suited to address the complexities of the multiple chronic diseases that are becoming increasingly prevalent.

At the other end of the age spectrum, millennials are now health care purchasers and consumers in their own right, and often display different wants and needs from preceding generations. Their preference for care "on their own time and in their own place" will impact the medical system. For at least some millennials, the increased focus and attention from concierge practices—together with the greater flexibility regarding time, place, and manner of access—will likely make them attractive.

Chapter 9

Concierge Medicine in the Future

Many different concierge models are springing up in health care in America. Direct primary care, "concierge lite," hybrid models, telemedicine health care, and home visitation health care are just a few examples. The public will determine which of these models will prevail. Certainly, access, cost, and high-quality service will be parameters on which the different models will be judged.

For those in traditional practices, higher expectations will also be applied. Refining the efficiency of caring for patients will minimize patients' desire to leave for concierge models. Quick service, politeness, a caring demeanor, and thoroughness will be required.

Parting Words

Much of this book is about common sense. Treat patients as you would want to be treated when you are ill, vulnerable, or frightened. Treat employees and fellow physicians as partners and teammates. One of my career mentors, Dr. John Fordtran, formed a medical advisory committee composed of physician representatives when he became chief of the medical department at Baylor University Medical Center in Dallas. He used this committee as a sounding board for physician issues; one such issue involved a physician who was reported for verbal abuse. A nurse working on a hospital floor had called the physician in the middle of the night for a laxative order. The doctor's response was not very polite, to say the least. The members of the committee, when asked for their opinions, mostly focused on defending the physician's perspective:

> "Laxative orders in the middle of the night can wait until morning."
> "The nurse could have given the laxative and then notified the doctor during daytime hours."
> "Nighttime nursing calls can be a nuisance."

Dr. Fordtran listened attentively and then asked the question, "Does anyone think that the nurse meant to purposefully annoy or irritate the physician?" The committee members all responded "no" but went on to accuse the nurse of having poor judgment and perhaps being naïve. He asked another question: "Would you have responded differently if the same question from the nurse took place at two o'clock in the afternoon?" Everyone agreed that such a question during the day would have been answered more favorably. He then concluded, "It sounds like you physicians need to arrange your schedules to take less calls so that you can be as polite to nurses at night as you are during the day."

It is never appropriate for a physician to talk condescendingly to a nurse, or, for that matter, to any employee, peer, or patient. Of course, physicians are also human. We are not immune to stress and irritability. It is important that we handle emotions in a manner that does not impact patient care or discredit our organizations, much less the profession.

Doing it right means being professional. Those of us who work in our craft represent the medical profession and should hold its standards high. Controlling one's emotions, when negative, is necessary. Humility is also useful. To paraphrase Timothy Radcliffe, "To be a [physician] requires two apparently contradictory qualities: confidence and humility" (BrainyQuote.com, 2017).

For physicians who are frustrated or burned out with modern medicine, the more relaxed pace of concierge models may be a good alternative. Senior physicians who want to slow down but not yet retire may also consider this different practice style. It should not be assumed, however, that a concierge practice necessarily entails less work; what it may provide is a different pace and more fulfilling work.

ADVANTAGES OF CONCIERGE PRACTICES

■ For Physicians
  - Less physician burnout
  - Prolonged careers
■ For Traditional Practices
  - Lessons from concierge models that can be translated to traditional practices
  - Higher expectations for quality, service, and safety
■ For Health Care Organizations
  - Cultivation of loyal patients and physicians
  - Potential for philanthropic donations

In closing, concierge practices allow close, accessible, trusting relationships with a physician, which may facilitate the diagnosis of medical problems and the completion of needed preventive services, and allow opportunities for better outcomes. Patients and physicians alike benefit from such relationships. There are added benefits for affiliated health care systems.

References

Adams, B. 2013. Nordstrom's: Where service is a culture, not a department. 27gen [cited June 8, 2017]. https://27gen.com/2013/08/06/nordstroms-where-service-is-a-culture-not-a-department/.

Advisory Board. 2017. Concierge care for all? Why MDVIP thinks the model makes sense for execs, teachers, and truck drivers [cited June 7, 2017]. https://www.advisory.com/daily-briefing/2015/06/10/interview-with-mdvip-ceo.

Albrecht, S. S., E. Mayer-Davis, and B. M. Popkin. 2017. Secular and race/ethnic trends in glycemic outcomes by BMI in US adults: The role of waist circumference. *Diabetes Metab Res Rev* no. 33 (5) doi:10.1002/dmrr.2889.

Alexander, J. A., L. R. Hearld, J. N. Mittler, and J. Harvey. 2012. Patient-physician role relationships and patient activation among individuals with chronic illness. *Health Serv Res* no. 47 (3 Pt 1): 1201–23. doi:10.1111/j.1475-6773.2011.01354.x.

American Academy of Private Physicians. 2017. About us [cited September 26, 2017]. https://www.facebook.com/pg/theAAPP/about/?ref=page_internal.

Anderson, P. B. 2014. *The Familiar Physician: Saving Your Doctor in the Era of Obamacare*. New York: Morgan James Publishing.

AthenaHealth. 2017. Meaningful use knowledge hub [cited June 7, 2017]. https://www.athenahealth.com/knowledge-hub/meaningful-use/what-is-meaningful-use.

Baird, A., M. F. Furukawa, B. Rahman, and E. S. Schneller. 2014. Corporate governance and the adoption of health information technology within integrated delivery systems. *Health Care Manage Rev* no. 39 (3):234–44. doi:10.1097/HMR.0b013e318294e5e6.

Beckman, H. B., and R. M. Frankel. 1984. The effect of physician behavior on the collection of data. *Ann Intern Med* no. 101 (5):692–6.

Berwick, D. M. 1996. A primer on leading the improvement of systems. *BMJ* no. 312 (7031):619–22.

Berwick, D. M., and A. D. Hackbarth. 2012. Eliminating waste in US health care. *JAMA* no. 307 (14):1513–6. doi:10.1001/jama.2012.362.

Birkmeyer, J. D., S. R. Finlayson, A. N. Tosteson, S. M. Sharp, A. L. Warshaw, and E. S. Fisher. 1999. Effect of hospital volume on in-hospital mortality with pancreaticoduodenectomy. *Surgery* no. 125 (3):250–6.

Block, A. M. 2015. Impatient patients. *Clinical Neurology News* [cited June 20, 2017]. http://www.mdedge.com/clinicalneurologynews/article/103901/impatient-patients.

BrainyQuote.com. 2017. Timothy Radcliffe quotes [cited June 21, 2017]. https://www.brainyquote.com/quotes/quotes/t/timothyrad260626.html.

Braunwald, E. 2013. Heart failure. *JACC Heart Fail* no. 1 (1): 1–20. doi:10.1016/j.jchf.2012.10.002.

Buttar, H. S., T. Li, and N. Ravi. 2005. Prevention of cardiovascular diseases: Role of exercise, dietary interventions, obesity and smoking cessation. *Exp Clin Cardiol* no. 10 (4):229–49.

Carrns, A. 2016. New cars are too expensive for the typical family, study finds. *New York Times* [cited May 12, 2017]. https://www.nytimes.com/2016/07/02/your-money/new-cars-are-too-expensive-for-the-typical-family-study-finds.html?_r=0.

Centers for Medicare and Medicaid Services. 2017a. Accountable care organizations (ACO) [cited June 21, 2017]. https://www.cms.gov/Medicare/Medicare-Fee-for-Service-Payment/ACO/.

Centers for Medicare and Medicaid Services. 2017b. Bundled Payments for Care Improvement (BPCI) Initiative: General information [cited June 7, 2017]. https://innovation.cms.gov/initiatives/bundled-payments/.

Centers for Medicare and Medicaid Services. 2017c. Hospital value-based purchasing program [cited June 29, 2017]. https://www.cms.gov/Medicare/Quality-Initiatives-Patient-Assessment-Instruments/hospital-value-based-purchasing/index.html?redirect=/hospital-value-based-purchasing.

Centers for Medicare and Medicaid Services. 2017d. Quality Payment Program [cited June 8, 2017]. https://qpp.cms.gov/.

Centers for Medicare and Medicaid Services. 2017e. Readmissions Reduction Program (HRRP) [cited June 29, 2017]. https://www.cms.gov/medicare/medicare-fee-for-service-payment/acuteinpatientpps/readmissions-reduction-program.html.

Chipkin, S. R., S. A. Klugh, and L. Chasan-Taber. 2001. Exercise and diabetes. *Cardiol Clin* no. 19 (3):489–505.

Christensen, C. M., J. Grossman, and J. Hwang. 2009. *The Innovator's Prescription*. New York: McGraw-Hill.

Colberg, S. R., R. J. Sigal, B. Fernhall, J. G. Regensteiner, B. J. Blissmer, R. R. Rubin, L. Chasan-Taber, A. L. Albright, B. Braun. 2010. Exercise and type 2 diabetes: The American College of Sports Medicine and the American Diabetes Association: joint position statement. *Diabetes Care* no. 33 (12):e147–67. doi:10.2337/dc10-9990.

Couch, C. 2016. *Accountable*. Boca Raton, FL: CRC Press.

Densen, P. 2011. Challenges and opportunities facing medical education. *Trans Am Clin Climatol Assoc* no. 122:48–58.

Dimick, J. B., P. J. Pronovost, J. A. Cowan, and P. A. Lipsett. 2003. Surgical volume and quality of care for esophageal resection: do high-volume hospitals have fewer complications? *Ann Thorac Surg* no. 75 (2):337–41.

Drucker Institute. 2013. *By Their Fruits Ye Shall Know Them* [cited June 20, 2017]. http://www.druckerinstitute.com/2013/04/by-their-fruits-ye-shall-know-them/.

Egan, B. M., D. T. Lackland, and D. W. Jones. 2010. Prehypertension: an opportunity for a new public health paradigm. *Cardiol Clin* no. 28 (4):561–9. doi:10.1016/j.ccl.2010.07.008.

Fact Tank. 2010. Baby Boomers retire. Pew Research Center [cited June 21, 2017]. http://www.pewresearch.org/fact-tank/2010/12/29/baby-boomers-retire/.

Feinberg, D., G. Steele, and A. Robeznieks. 2015. Aiming to provide concierge care "for the masses". *Mod Healthc* no. 45 (37):30–1.

Finkelstein, C. 2017. Improving physician resiliency. AMA's Practice Improvement Strategies. STEPS Forward™ [cited June 8, 2017]. https://www.stepsforward.org/modules/improving-physician-resilience.

Fischer, S. 2015. Patient choice and consumerism in healthcare: Only a mirage of wishful thinking? In *Challenges and Opportunities in Health Care Management*, edited by S. Gurtner and K. Soyez, 173–84. Cham, Switzerland: Springer.

Fleming-Dutra, K. E., R. Mangione-Smith, and L. A. Hicks. 2016. How to prescribe fewer unnecessary antibiotics: Talking points that work with patients and their families. *Am Fam Physician* no. 94 (3):200–2.

Gallo, A. 2014. The value of keeping the right customers. *Harvard Business Review* [cited June 8, 2017]. https://hbr.org/2014/10/the-value-of-keeping-the-right-customers.

Gaskins, N. D., P. D. Sloane, C. M. Mitchell, A. Ammerman, S. B. Ickes, and C. S. Williams. 2007. Poor nutritional habits: A modifiable predecessor of chronic illness? A North Carolina Family Medicine Research Network (NC-FM-RN) study. *J Am Board Fam Med* no. 20 (2):124–34. doi:10.3122/jabfm.2007.02.060151.

Geneen, H., and A. Moscow. 1985. *Managing.* London: Granada Publishing Ltd.

Goldman, L., and E. F. Cook. 1984. The decline in ischemic heart disease mortality rates. An analysis of the comparative effects of medical interventions and changes in lifestyle. *Ann Intern Med* no. 101 (6):825–36.

Goroll, A. H. 2015. Toward trusting therapeutic relationships: -In favor of the annual physical. *N Engl J Med* no. 373 (16):1487–9. doi:10.1056/NEJMp1508270.

Greene, J., J. H. Hibbard, R. Sacks, V. Overton, and C. D. Parrotta. 2015. When patient activation levels change, health outcomes and costs change, too. *Health Aff (Millwood)* no. 34 (3):431–7. doi:10.1377/hlthaff.2014.0452.

Greenhalgh, T., R. Snow, S. Ryan, S. Rees, and H. Salisbury. 2015. Six "biases" against patients and carers in evidence-based medicine. *BMC Med* no. 13:200. doi:10.1186/s12916-015-0437-x.

Gunderman, R. 2016. The case for concierge medicine. *The Atlantic* [cited November 14, 2016]. http://www.theatlantic.com/health/archive/2014/07/the-case-for-concierge-medicine/374296/.

Ha, J. F., and N. Longnecker. 2010. Doctor–patient communication: A review. *Ochsner J* no. 10 (1):38–43.

Hartmans, A., and N. McAlone. 2016. The story of how Travis Kalanick built Uber into the most feared and valuable startup in the world. *Business Insider* [cited June 8, 2017]. http://www.businessinsider.com/ ubers-history/#june-1998-scour-a-peer-to-peer-search-engine-startup-that-kalanick-had-dropped-out-of-ucla-to-join-snags-its-first-investment-from-former-disney-president-michael-ovitz-and-ron-burkle-of-yucaipa-companies-1.

HealthIT.gov. 2017. EHR incentives & certification: Meaningful Use definition & objectives [cited June 29, 2017]. https://www.healthit.gov/providers-professionals/ meaningful-use-definition-objectives.

HealthTexas Provider Network. 2016. HealthTexas Provider Network: A team approach to patient care [cited November 14, 2016]. http://www.healthtexas.com.

Hertz, B. T. 2014. Antibiotic requests: Tips for physicians dealing with patient demands. *Modern Medicine Network* [cited June 20, 2017]. http://medicaleconomics.modernmedicine.com/med-ical-economics/content/tags/antibiotic/antibiotic-requests-tips-physicians-dealing-patient-demand?page=full.

Hornik, C. P., X. He, J. P. Jacobs, J. S. Li, R. D. Jaquiss, M. L. Jacobs, S. M. O'Brien, K. Welke, E. D. Peterson, and S. K. Pasquali. 2012. Relative impact of surgeon and center volume on early mortality after the Norwood operation. *Ann Thorac Surg* no. 93 (6):1992–7. doi:10.1016/j.athoracsur.2012.01.107.

Hwang, W., J. Chang, M. Laclair, and H. Paz. 2013. Effects of integrated delivery system on cost and quality. *Am J Manag Care* no. 19 (5):e175–84.

Johnson, D. K., and S. Stern. 2016. Five secrets of customer-obsessed cultures [cited June 15, 2017]. https://www.for-rester.com/report/Five+Secrets+Of+CustomerObsessed+Cultu res/-/E-RES130984.

JustDisney.com. 2017. Walt Disney quotes [cited June 8, 2017]. http://www.justdisney.com/walt_disney/quotes/index.html.

Klemes, A., R. E. Seligmann, L. Allen, M. A. Kubica, K. Warth, and B. Kaminetsky. 2012. Personalized preventive care leads to significant reductions in hospital utilization. *Am J Manag Care* no. 18 (12):e453–60.

Komaroff, A. L. September 2009. Executive physicals: What's the ROI? *Harvard Business Review.*

Lavizzo-Mourey, R. 2012. We must focus on preventing disease if we want our nation to thrive. *The Atlantic* [cited June 21, 2017]. https://www.theatlantic.com/health/archive/2012/05/we-must-focus-on-preventing-disease-if-we-want-our-nation-to-thrive/257759/.

Lee, T. H. 2016. *An Epidemic of Empathy in Healthcare: How to Deliver Compassionate, Connected Patient Care that Creates a Competitive Advantage.* New York: McGraw-Hill Education.

Lee, T. H., and T. Cosgrove. 2014. Engaging Doctors in the Healthcare Revolution. *Harvard Bus Rev* no. 92:104–111.

Lipp, D. 2013. *Disney U: How Disney University Develops the World's Most Engaged, Loyal, and Customer-Centric Employees.* New York: McGraw-Hill.

Long, M. 2012. Health law's survival means more demand for fewer doctors. *The Wall Street Journal* [cited November 14, 2016]. http://blogs.wsj.com/health/2012/06/28/health-laws-survival-means-more-demand-for-fewer-doctors/.

Lown, B. 1999. *The Lost Art of Healing: Practicing Compassion in Medicine.* New York: Ballantine Books.

Lushniak, B. D., D. E. Alley, B. Ulin, and C. Graffunder. 2015. The National Prevention Strategy: Leveraging multiple sectors to improve population health. *Am J Public Health* no. 105 (2):229–31. doi:10.2105/AJPH.2014.302257.

Lutz, A. 2014. Nordstrom's employee handbook has only one rule. *Business Insider* [cited June 8, 2017]. http://www.businessinsider.com/nordstroms-employee-handbook-2014-10.

MacDonald, I. 2017. High-end, high-cost concierge medicine for America's wealthiest widens healthcare divide [cited June 29, 2017]. http://www.fiercehealthcare.com/healthcare/high-end-high-cost-concierge-medicine-for-america-s-wealthiest-widens-healthcare-divide.

Madara, J. L., and J. Burkhart. 2015. Professionalism, self-regulation, and motivation: How did health care get this so wrong? *JAMA* no. 313 (18):1793–4. doi:10.1001/jama.2015.4045.

Matthews, M. 2015. Doctors face: a huge Medicare and Medicaid pay cut in 2015. *Forbes* [cited June 7, 2017]. https://www.forbes.com/sites/merrillmatthews/2015/01/05/doctors-face-a-huge-medicare-and-medicaid-pay-cut-in-2015/#40e1eeee3173.

Matthias, M. S., E. E. Krebs, A. A. Bergman, J. M. Coffing, and M. J. Bair. 2014. Communicating about opioids for chronic pain: a qualitative study of patient attributions and the influence of the patient-physician relationship. *Eur J Pain* no. 18 (6):835–43.

MD2. 2017. *Press: Is Paying for Concierge Health Care Worth it?* [cited June 7, 2017]. http://www.md2.com/press/is-paying-for-concierge-health-care-worth-it.

MDVIP. 2017. [cited June 7, 2017]. http://www.mdvip.com/.

Menke, A., S. Casagrande, L. Geiss, and C. C. Cowie. 2015. Prevalence of and trends in diabetes among adults in the United States, 1988–2012. *JAMA* no. 314 (10):1021–9. doi:10.1001/jama.2015.10029.

Merriam-Webster Dictionary. 2017. Compliance [cited June 7, 2017]. https://www.merriam-webster.com/dictionary/compliance.

Merriam-Webster Dictionary. 2017. Consumerism [cited June 8, 2017]. https://www.merriam-webster.com/dictionary/consumerism.

Merriam-Webster Learner's Dictionary. 2017. Uber [cited June 8, 2017]. http://www.learnersdictionary.com/definition/uber-.

Mikkelson, D. 2007. Humorous inflight announcements. *Snopes* [cited June 29, 2017]. http://www.snopes.com/travel/airline/announce.asp.

Moser, M. 1983. A decade of progress in the management of hypertension. *Hypertension* no. 5 (6):808–13.

Munro, D. 2016. Annual healthcare cost for family of four now at $25,826 [cited June 21, 2017]. https://www.forbes.com/sites/danmunro/2016/05/24/annual-healthcare-cost-for-family-of-four-now-at-25826/#37c83a511f52.

Musich, S., A. Klemes, M. A. Kubica, S. Wang, and K. Hawkins. 2014. Personalized preventive care reduces healthcare expenditures among Medicare Advantage beneficiaries. *Am J Manag Care* no. 20 (8):613–20.

Musich, S., S. Wang, K. Hawkins, and A. Klemes. 2016. The impact of personalized preventive care on health care quality, utilization, and expenditures. *Popul Health Manag* no. 19 (6):389–397. doi:10.1089/pop.2015.0171.

Myers, J. 2003. Cardiology patient pages: Exercise and cardiovascular health. *Circulation* no. 107 (1):e2–5.

National Center for Health Statistics. 2017. FastFacts: Osteoporosis [cited June 21, 2017]. https://www.cdc.gov/nchs/fastats/osteoporosis.htm.

Nazario, R. J. 2012. The "patient experience": Is it patient pandering? *Today's Hospitalist* [cited June 20, 2017]. http://www.todayshospitalist.com/Thepatient-experience-Is-it-patient-pandering/.

Office of Energy Efficiency and Renewable Energy. 2017. Vehicle Technologies Office: Advanced combustion engines [cited June 8, 2017]. https://energy.gov/eere/vehicles/vehicle-technologies-office-advanced-combustion-engines.

Piotroski, J. D., and S. Srinivasan. 2008. Regulation and bonding: The Sarbanes-Oxley Act and the flow of international listings. *J Account Res* no. 46 (2):383–425.

Portman, R. M., and K. Romanow. 2008. Concierge medicine: Legal issues, ethical dilemmas, and policy challenges. *J Health Life Sci Law* no. 1 (3):1, 3–38.

Press Ganey. 2017. About Press Ganey [cited June 15, 2017]. http://www.pressganey.com/about.

Reichheld, F. F., and T. Teal. 2001. *The Loyalty Effect: The Hidden Force Behind Growth, Profits, and Lasting Value.* Boston, MA: Harvard Business School Press.

Ritz-Carlton. 2017. Gold Standards [cited June 8, 2017]. http://www.ritzcarlton.com/en/about/gold-standards.

Robinson, R. K. 2017. President, Baylor Health Care System Foundation. Personal communication, July 7.

Rubin, R. 2014. AIDET® in the medical practice: More important than ever. Studer Group [cited June 20, 2017]. https://www.studergroup.com/resources/articles-and-industry-updates/insights/november-2014/aidet-in-the-medical-practice-more-important-than.

Schein, E. H. 1985. *Organizational Culture and Leadership.* San Francisco, CA: Jossey-Bass.

Schwartz, N. D. 2017. The doctor is in. Co-pay? $40,000. *The New York Times* [cited June 29, 2017]. https://mobile.nytimes.com/2017/06/03/business/economy/high-end-medical-care.html.

Scripps. 2017. Concierge medicine [cited June 7, 2017]. https://www.scripps.org/services/concierge-medicine.

Sculco, A. D., D. C. Paup, B. Fernhall, and M. J. Sculco. 2001. Effects of aerobic exercise on low back pain patients in treatment. *Spine J* no. 1 (2):95–101.

Sealover, E. 2012. DaVita opens Denver health care office. *Denver Business Journal* [cited June 7, 2017]. http://www.bizjournals.com/denver/news/2012/09/12/davita-opens-denver-health-care-office.html.

Sewell, C., and P. B. Brown. 2002. *Customers for Life: How to Turn that One-Time Buyer into a Lifetime Customer.* New York: Doubleday.

Shanafelt, T. D., and J. H. Noseworthy. 2017. Executive leadership and physician well-being: Nine organizational strategies to promote engagement and reduce burnout. *Mayo Clin Proc* no. 92 (1):129–146. doi:10.1016/j.mayocp.2016.10.004.

Signature MD. 2017. What is the executive physical for concierge medicine? [cited June 7, 2017]. http://signaturemd.com/executive-physical-concierge-medicine/.

Sloan, A. 2017. What is Uber's stock really worth? Who knows? *The Washington Post,* September 1 [cited November 11, 2017]. https://www.washingtonpost.com/business/economy/what-is-ubers-share-price-really-worth-who-knows/2017/09/01/e496adde-8e5d-11e7-84c0-02cc069f2c37_story.html.

Society of General Internal Medicine. 2017. Becoming a general internist [cited June 21, 2017]. http://www.sgim.org/career-center/proudtobegim/learn-about-gim.

Spector, R., and P. D. McCarthy. 2012. *The Nordstrom Way to Customer Service Excellence: The Handbook for Becoming the "Nordstrom" of Your Industry.* 2nd ed. Hoboken, NJ: John Wiley and Sons.

Studer Group. 2017. AIDET® Patient communication [cited June 20, 2017]. https://www.studergroup.com/aidet.

Terry, K. 2011. Health IT: The glue for accountable care organizations—Four big systems show how they're using EHRs, connectivity, and data warehouses to drive ACOs. *Healthc Inform* no. 28 (5):16, 18, 20 passim.

Terry, K. 2015. Physicians and telehealth: Is it time to embrace virtual visits? *Med Econ* no. 92 (13):48–52.

The Advisory Board Company. 2016. Assessing the case for concierge medicine: Strategic and operational insights for medical group executives considering retainer-based practice models.

The Commonwealth Fund. 2017. Mirror, mirror on the wall, 2014 update: How the U.S. health care system compares internationally [cited June 30, 2017]. http://www.commonwealthfund.org/publications/fund-reports/2014/jun/mirror-mirror.

The Physicians Foundation. 2016. The Physicians Foundation 2016 Patient Survey [cited June 29, 2017]. http://www.physiciansfoundation.org/news/the-physicians-foundation-2016-patient-survey.

The Statistics Portal. 2017. Automotive electronics cost as a percentage of total car cost worldwide from 1950 to 2030 [cited June 8, 2017]. https://www.statista.com/statistics/277931/automotive-electronics-cost-as-a-share-of-total-car-cost-worldwide/.

UC San Diego Health. 2017. Concierge medicine [cited June 7, 2017]. https://health.ucsd.edu/specialties/primary-care/concierge-medicine/Pages/default.aspx.

Ventola, C. L. 2015. The antibiotic resistance crisis: Part 1—Causes and threats. *P T* no. 40 (4):277–83.

Virginia Mason. 2017. Concierge medicine [cited June 7, 2017]. https://www.virginiamason.org/concierge-medicine.

Wachter, R. M. 2016. Presentation to the Texas Care Alliance.

Walt Disney World Resort. 2017. Walt Disney World fun facts [cited June 8, 2017]. http://wdwnews.com/fact-sheets/2014/10/31/walt-disney-world-fun-facts/.

Winter, F. D., Jr. 2001. Baylor Health Care System quality initiatives: A view from the HealthTexas Provider Network. *Proc (Bayl Univ Med Cent)* no. 14 (4):442–5; discussion 445–6.

Yang, T. 2016. Telehealth parity laws. *Health Affairs* [cited June 21, 2017]. http://www.healthaffairs.org/healthpolicybriefs/brief.php?brief_id=162.

Index

9781138035584